winner takes all

Seven-and-a-half principles for winning more bids, tenders, pitches and proposals

SCOTT KEYSER

Published by
LID Publishing Limited
The Record Hall, Studio 204,
16-16a Baldwins Gardens,
London EC1N 7RJ, UK

524 Broadway, 11th Floor, Suite 08-120,
New York, NY 10012, US

info@lidpublishing.com
www.lidpublishing.com

A member of:

BPR
Business Publishers Roundtable
www.businesspublishersroundtable.com

© Scott Keyser, 2018
© LID Publishing Limited, 2018
First edition published in 2014

Printed in Great Britain by TJ International
ISBN: 978-1-911498-89-6

Cover and page design: Matthew Renaudin

winner
takes all

Seven-and-a-half
principles for winning
more bids, tenders,
pitches and proposals

SCOTT KEYSER

LONDON   NEW YORK   SHANGHAI
MADRID   BARCELONA   BOGOTA
MEXICO CITY   MONTERREY   BUENOS AIRES

FOR BETH BENNETT

CONTENTS

PROLOGUE

I recall many moons ago sitting in a restaurant in Waterloo, London, having lunch with my bid team colleagues.

At the head of the table sat our boss, Beth Bennett, Head of National Proposals at Ernst & Young. A tall, gaunt American with a huge heart, Beth was in the throes of transforming the firm's bids, tenders and proposals.

But the atmosphere was subdued. We'd recently finished a marathon of a re-proposal for a huge contract to audit a pharmaceutical company. Nine long months, several US trips, numerous client conference calls and lots of midnight candles later, we were exhausted and relieved it was all over. But we didn't know if we'd retained the contract or not and the call from the client was imminent.

In the middle of the meal, Beth took a call from Washington on her mobile. Conversations stopped; knives and forks were rested on plates. After the usual pleasantries, the colour drained from Beth's face and tears started to stream down her cheeks. She put the phone down and looked at us all. Then she clenched her fist and punched the air, uttering her stock phrase, 'Man, oh man!'.

We'd retained the contract.

The client said it was the best business document he'd ever seen, they would use it as an instruction manual to run the contract, and it had raised the bar for future tender responses from suppliers.

It felt like a massive victory, but all we'd done was fight to keep a contract. Beth's tears were not just tears of relief, but also of elation and pride in her team.

At that point, we'd all have willingly followed Beth into battle.

BACKGROUND TO
WINNER TAKES ALL

My journey through the landscape of proposals and business development (BD) started in March 1994 when I joined Ernst & Young as a
grand-sounding 'National Proposals Consultant'. I'd been having a ball
in London and Melbourne as a freelance copywriter writing recruitment
press ads, product brochures, user manuals, newsletters and the odd radio
commercial. But the 1990/91 recession hit me hard, so I decided to come
in from the cold.

Recommended to Ernst & Young's Head of Proposals by the sister of a
good friend, I found myself working in a small but perfectly formed team
of five people whose mandate was to help practice teams in the firm bid
for and win major tenders. This mission was part of a broader campaign
to make the firm more sales-oriented, including turning service lines like
audit from a commodity into a distinctive business tool.

Beth was Head of Proposals; her brief was to take the firm's bids and
tenders to the next level. She believed passionately in what she did and
spread the word about her team and the value we could add. Naturally shy, she became an Emmeline Pankhurst on the subject of proposals,
fighting our cause, protecting us when we were exhausted and overloaded with bids, bashing partners' heads together when necessary and im-
pressing them with her insights into an opportunity, a team selection or
a document section.

We worked tirelessly. Ninety-hour weeks were common. Internal and
external audit, corporate finance, tax, management consulting – after
months of Beth's evangelizing, we had people banging our door down to
enrol us in their bid. They knew that they stood a much better chance of
winning with us than without us. So we saw the entire tendering process,
from start to finish, through the filter of different industry sectors, service
lines and teams.

We learnt on the job, resilience forged in the white heat of the tendering process. At our height, we were advising partners on the bid/no bid decision; pre-submission client meetings; team selection; win-themes; drafting, editing, design and production of the document; design, preparation and delivery of the oral presentation; and post-proposal research.

Eighteen months later, the UK firm's tender win-rate had doubled. I'm not saying National Proposals should take all the plaudits for that, but we certainly helped.

You will have gathered that Ernst & Young was a formative experience for me, moulding my view of the tendering process. Inevitably, I absorbed that learning and have added to it in the ensuing years as an independent BD consultant and trainer, building on it with successive layers of experience like geological strata.

Fast forward to 2018 and this second edition. What's changed in the BD world? Sadly, not much.

Bidders are still not pre-qualifying opportunities robustly, bidding for anything that moves. Their BD teams are proposal factories, where the emphasis is not on quality but on getting the bid 'out the door' to work on the next one.

Among professional services firms especially, there's a tendency to over-emphasize the bid document, at the expense of communicating with the client pre-submission.

Another abiding issue is bidders talking more about themselves than about the client. I call this 'we-ing' all over the client. The words 'we', 'us' and 'our' outnumber the magic words 'you' and 'your'. The message is, "We're more important than you."

Allied to the 'we-ing' issue is that too many bidders don't know the client well enough, so struggle to tailor their response to the individual decision-makers' specific needs. This may be because they haven't put the work in to define their 'avatar', or ideal client. The result is bland, generic proposals.

Finally, in the merciless glare of tendering for business, another issue has come to light. Maybe it was there all along, but now I see it everywhere. It's that most bidders haven't nailed their value proposition – their unique offer to the market. This second edition doesn't tackle value propositions head-on (my next book?) but, if you follow my advice, especially Principle 3, you'll be halfway there.

So, if you're in BD and want to win more business, I'm glad to say this book is still relevant to you.

HOW TO USE THIS BOOK

My 26 years of working on bids have spawned the seven and a half principles of proposals best practice that this book is about.

If you have any experience of tendering, none of the principles should confuse or surprise you. They're generic, so they can be used in virtually any industry. But it's how you apply them that determines whether a bid is won or lost. So, in the pages that follow, I will share under each principle what's worked for me and what hasn't.

This is my take on proposals best practice for your benefit, so that you know how high the bar is and how to reach it. Of course, it would be unrealistic – and probably inappropriate – to expect to reproduce every aspect of best practice for every bid. But I want you to fill your tendering toolkit with as many useful instruments as you can and know which ones to use when.

WELCOME NEWCOMERS!

If you're new to tendering, thank you for picking up this book.

Maybe you've just joined Sales & Marketing, BD or Proposals and you need to grasp the basics quickly. If you want to make an immediate impact on your new team and the other stakeholders in the business that you'll engage with on bids, I suggest you get to grips with three aspects of tendering.

First, you need to understand the process governing how private, public and voluntary sector contracts are tendered and let. Second, find out about the core principles of best practice if you want to win more bids than you lose. And third, get familiar with the language and terminology that is bandied about in Proposals Land (you don't want to look blank when someone says 'restricted procedure', 'RFP' or 'value proposition').

The principles of this book follow the logical order of the bidding process. So if you only read the chapter headings and the summaries at the start of each chapter, you'll get a sense of the flow of the process. Then you can decide which particular stages of the process interest you, or the ones you need to know about for your job, and read those in more detail.

Ultimately, I recommend you read the book from cover to cover. But I would say that, wouldn't I?

If you flick through the glossary at the back of the book, you'll also find what I consider to be the tendering terms you should be familiar with if you want to be credible in this field. And 'credible' is a vital word if you're working in any bid support role.

Whatever path you take through this book, my goal for you is this: when you make your first contribution to a bid, I want your colleagues, internal customers or external clients to sit up and take notice.

WELCOME EXPERIENCED BIDDERS!

If you're not new to tendering, you're likely to be seeking something different.

You may want to complete your mastery of the craft of tendering. Or perhaps you want to bring your team up to your level of expertise. Specifically, you may want to use this book to help you:

- Pre-qualify opportunities more robustly (**Principle 1**)
- Get a new angle on team selection (**Principle 2**)
- Personalize your bid to each of the five typical buying roles (**Principle 2**)
- Out-fox the competition before you've even put pen to paper (**Principle 3**)
- Structure any free-form proposal for maximum impact (**Principles 3 and 4**)
- Use the written word as a competitive weapon (**Principle 4**)
- Produce compelling executive summaries (**Principle 4.5**)
- Pitch with power (and coach others to do the same) (**Principle 5**)
- Get candid, useful feedback from the client (**Principle 6**)
- Manage bids better (**Principle 7**)

Whatever your situation, I've tried to make the book as 'real world' as possible; hence the number of times you'll see the phrase 'How to…'. It's short on theory and long on practice. Relevance is also a goal, which is why each chapter closes with an exercise called 'Food for Thought'. I want you to relate whatever I've said in that chapter to your own experience and context, so you gain insights and ideas that you can apply to your very next bid.

It may only take one good idea well executed to transform your win-rate.

Whether you're a novice or a veteran, my ultimate goal is to help you win more contracts, instructions, commissions or mandates more efficiently and with less stress on you and your organization.

So it matters not if you head up BD, Sales or Proposals in a multi-national, a partnership or an SME, if you're an overworked bid manager or proposals writer, an internal or an external consultant. Whoever you are, whatever industry you're in and wherever you are in the tendering process, there's something here for you.

Yours tenderly,

Scott

principle

1

Pre-qualify every opportunity

CHAPTER SUMMARY

1. What pre-qualification is and what it's not.
2. The benefits of pre-qualifying and the risks of not doing so.
3. How to pre-qualify properly.
4. Exercise to assess how well you pre-qualify.

P re-qualifying a bid or tender opportunity is the first vital step in the process, but it's rarely done. And, when it is, it's usually done badly. Yet **by learning to say no to more bids than yes, you'll boost your win-rate.** When my clients get this paradox, their win-rate almost always goes up.

SO WHAT IS 'PRE-QUALIFICATION'?

It's an internal process for deciding whether or not to respond to an invitation to tender (ITT) or request for proposal (RFP). When you pre-qualify an opportunity, you analyse all the reasons why you should bid and why you shouldn't, then weigh them up to reach a Bid/No Bid decision.

It's often referred to as an 'opportunity analysis' or 'cost-benefit analysis'. You're assessing what it will cost you to bid – in terms of (wo)manpower, management time, materials and resources, distraction from or neglect of existing clients, turning away other opportunities – in return for the potential benefits of winning the tender and delivering the contract.

(By the way, don't confuse this with a 'PQQ', or pre-qualification questionnaire. This is the first stage in the two-stage UK public sector 'restricted' tendering procedure. It's a form that all interested suppliers must complete. The buying organization (formally known as the 'contracting authority') uses this information to assess the supplier's suitability for the contract and weed out the unsuitable ones, for reasons of capacity, financial standing or relevant experience. This means they don't waste their time assessing non-starter bids for a popular contract that may attract lots of interest from hopeful but inappropriate suppliers. The PQQ helps the buying organization narrow the field before issuing a formal ITT to a select group of bidders. It assesses the bidder, not the bid.)

WHAT HAPPENS WHEN YOU DON'T PRE-QUALIFY?

In every economic downturn I've lived through, I've observed the same syndrome in the BD world: a panic-stricken compulsion to bid for every opportunity available.

And the research I've run among BD professionals around the world confirms this. Their biggest gripe is being told by their superiors to bid for any opportunity that comes along. "Let's take a punt!" – "Let's wing it!" – "It could be massive!" – are familiar refrains from naïve managers or over-enthusiastic sales people. The problem with this approach is that there's no distinction between winnable and unwinnable opportunities. I call it 'proposals machismo' and it brings at least nine risks that can wreck your business:

BIG FAT RISK #1:
YOU WASTE LIMITED RESOURCES, INCLUDING THE GOODWILL OF YOUR BD TEAM

Responding to a tender – especially an onerous one with lots of questions to answer or hoops to jump through – demands high levels of energy, time, money and attention. (I once helped a major construction company respond to a public sector tender with 90 questions, many of which overlapped, but all of which demanded well-researched, comprehensive answers. Nightmare.) These resources are finite, so it's your duty to your shareholders, investors, directors, managers or employees to use them wisely.

Winning tenders also demands huge commitment from your BD team. Forcing them to bid for unwinnable opportunities stretches their goodwill, sometimes to breaking point. Why should they give their best, if they know there's scant chance of winning? You need your bid team running that extra mile for you, not dragging their heels.

And we neglect at our peril the impact on people's morale, confidence and self-esteem of losing more bids than they win, thanks to a poor or non-existent pre-qualification process.

BIG FAT RISK #2:
YOU MISS EASIER, MORE WINNABLE OPPORTUNITIES

It's cheaper and easier to sell to existing clients than gain new ones. Your time and energy could be better spent developing relationships with your existing clients – to up-sell or cross-sell more products or services

– than engaging in a time-consuming tender for a new client. Which opportunities will give you the best return on your investment of time, energy and resources?

BIG FAT RISK #3:
OPPORTUNITY COST

This is the cost to your organization of bidding for a particular opportunity – not in terms of the resources you devote to it, but in terms of the alternatives you must forgo when faced with mutually exclusive choices.

Diverting resources to a major bid may cause you to neglect existing clients or programmes; the value of that neglect is your 'opportunity cost'. When pre-qualifying any opportunity, the challenge is to understand the total cost to your organization of bidding for it. This includes the value of the opportunities you have to pass on as well as the resources you will spend to respond to it.

BIG FAT RISK #4:
YOUR BD TEAM BECOMES A PROPOSALS FACTORY

When you fail to pre-qualify, you're constantly reacting to opportunities that suddenly appear, usually with demanding and unrealistic deadlines. So you heap more and more pressure on your bid team, flooding them with a relentless stream of bids. The result? Demotivated, dispirited and exhausted staff, whose sole aim is not to create tailored, compelling responses, but to just get the bid 'out the door' and onto the next one.

The 'proposals factory' or 'production line' is the most common syndrome I see in the BD world.

BIG FAT RISK #5:
LIKE YOUR TEAM, YOUR PROPOSALS BECOME TIRED

Because of Risk #4, you don't have time to tailor the bid to the client, so you copy and paste from the last proposal, including doing a 'find and replace' on the client's name! Your submissions become predictable, generic and dull to the client, because they haven't been written with their business needs, culture or decision-makers in mind.

BIG FAT RISK #6:
YOU MISS WARNING SIGNS IN THE CLIENT'S BEHAVIOUR

Because you're so fixated on submitting a response, you choose to ignore risks like long payment terms, muddled decision-making or dodgy ethics.

STORY

The head of BD in an international oil and gas company recently told me that his company were hell-bent on responding to a huge tender issued by a state-owned gas company, despite the client's resistance to answering their clarification questions (alarm bells should have been ringing). When the client asked for in-depth technical ideas to solve a particular problem, the local BD managers in his organization were so desperate to win that they ended up giving away half their intellectual property (IP) – and still losing.

BIG FAT RISK #7:
YOU BECOME A SERIAL 'FAILER' OF BIDS

This is not uncommon in local authority tenders, where a local supplier may repeatedly fail in its bid for contracts outside its specialism or capacity. The risk here is that it may not be invited to bid for future, more winnable contracts and find itself excluded from its local market.

BIG FAT RISK #8:
YOUR TENDERING ROI GOES SOUTH

If you spread yourself too thin, the overall quality of your submissions is likely to fall. This generates its own vicious circle: as your win-rate drops, there's more pressure on you to respond to more bids to compensate for the losses. And if you're not expanding your BD function to cope with the growing demand, your win-rate will continue to fall. This means the return on investment (ROI) on your tendering activity will be low, if not negative.

You want a rising return on your tendering investment, so senior management sees your BD team not as a cost centre, but as a wealth-generator or value-adder. And, if you achieve that as Head of BD, you're more likely to get a seat at the top table of your organization.

BIG FAT RISK #9:
YOU GET NASTY SURPRISES

Finally, if you fail to pre-qualify properly and enter the fray with your eyes closed, you may discover glaring gaps in your knowledge, experience, capability or value proposition halfway through the process – but by then you're committed and it's too late to do anything about it, barring an ignominious withdrawal. Investing time and energy in pre-qualifying an opportunity is like planning in the writing process. It initially feels like a waste of time, as if you're spinning your wheels. But when you start drafting and it flows smoothly because you've clarified your structure, purpose and main messages, then you realize it wasn't wasted time at all, but a vital step in the process that will save you time and energy farther down the track.

So pre-qualifying every opportunity – thinking hard about how attractive, winnable and deliverable it really is – can save us from proposals insanity, exhaustion, heartache, divorce and mental breakdown. I remember seeing a senior manager for one of my clients, overloaded with his day-job and leading a massive bid, fall apart in a meeting. It wasn't pretty and acted as a salutary reminder of how stressful a winnable bid can be, let alone one that doesn't have your name on it.

WHY DON'T MOST ORGANIZATIONS PRE-QUALIFY?

Because they're scared of missing an opportunity. Or because the sales culture of their organization is to chase everything. Or because they're missing their sales targets and are starting to panic. Or because they think that if they throw enough mud at the wall, some of it has to stick.

Trouble is, they're not throwing mud. They're throwing money, time, management attention and other finite resources. If they worked out what it costs them to submit a bid, they'd get a shock.

Have I convinced you yet of the need to pre-qualify?

HOW DO YOU PRE-QUALIFY PROPERLY?

First of all, you need to call a meeting of all the main stakeholders in the particular opportunity, e.g. the person who will lead the bid, the core bid team and the account manager, or whoever has been tasked with building a relationship with the client. You might also consider inviting other people in your organization not directly involved in the bid, but who know the client or have had contact with them, such as fee earners who may have worked with another part of the organization. The purpose of this 'pre-qual' meeting is to pool everything you know about the client so that you can make an informed Bid/No Bid decision.

STORY

I was once involved in a tender opportunity where a relatively junior person had some insight, through a social contact, into the client CEO's attitude to Ernst & Young. It turned out that he'd had a bad experience with a local office in the past and this had coloured his view of the whole firm.

When it came down to our Bid/No Bid decision, which was very marginal, after some quite heated discussion, this inside knowledge tipped the scales towards not proceeding.

A few years later, when that particular CEO had left, we won a contract with the same organization. In a chance conversation over a beer one evening, one of their directors confirmed that Ernst & Young would never have won that contract with the former CEO in post. 'Over my dead body' seemed to have been his general sentiment. This vindicated what at the time had been a traumatic internal decision for the bid team allocated to that opportunity.

The pre-qualification meeting must be positioned and scheduled as an important commitment in people's diaries. It's much more than a quick chat around the coffee machine or an afterthought to another meeting. The bid manager's job is to persuade sceptical colleagues that, in the long run, investing a little time up-front could save them loads of time and money.

There are several ways to pre-qualify, but here are two. One is *conceptual* and encourages you to assess four 'abilities': is the opportunity winn**able**, desir**able**, deliver**able** and profit**able**?

The other is *numerical*, where you score different elements of the opportunity. This is shown later in this chapter as a numerical form that gives you a total score for reasons to bid and reasons not to bid, with a 'bid zone' at the end that indicates what your decision should be.

You may choose to combine the two, i.e. create a numerical form for each of the four conceptual 'abilities' listed above and described in detail below. Either way, I'm sure you'll want to tailor your own pre-qualification tool to your particular team, organization, industry and/or sector.

A CONCEPTUAL TAKE ON PRE-QUALIFICATION
(THE FOUR 'ABILITIES')

WINNABILITY
For clarity, I've broken this ability down into four areas: track record/ capability, team, relationship and competition.

Track record/capability:
- Do you have recent and relevant experience in the particular type of work that the contract demands?
- Have you done similar jobs successfully?
- Can you provide superb, relevant references from delighted clients?

If the client is risk-averse, showing that you're a safe pair of hands with their type of work is essential. That's why buyers want to see evidence of your claims, rather than marketing fluff.

Team:
Research conducted at Ernst & Young found that clients buy the team before the organization. Making it clear that you're putting your best people on the team shows the client that you're committed to winning and to doing the best possible job.
- Can you field the best team for the particular client, as opposed to the one merely available?
- Do you have the resources or 'band-width' to bid?
- Will the right subject matter experts be available at the right time to contribute?
- Is the ideal bid leader going to be available throughout the tender or will they be on annual leave at a critical point in the process?

Relationship with the client:
How well you know and get on with the client are vital factors in your success or failure. Bidders that don't have a pre-existing relationship with most of the client decision-makers will have a hard time building that rapport under the pressure of the tendering process.

If you're going in cold, you'll have to work hard to gain their trust, especially if access to them is limited. And if a competitor is already in there, dislodging them could be hard. The client may find the idea of switching to a new supplier just too painful, uncertain and risky. Several of my clients simply won't bid if they don't already have a strong relationship with the buying organization.

- Does the client know you, like you and trust you?
- Can you 'level-sell', i.e. match your team members with their opposite number in the client?
- Is access to the client open, limited or even denied altogether?
- Do you know them well enough to be able to identify each decision-maker's agenda?

Competition:
- Do you know how many other bidders you're up against?
- Do you know the strengths and weaknesses of the other bidders?

If the field is large and you're making up the numbers, think twice – especially if the client doesn't know you or you have no track record to point to.

DESIRABILITY
- Does the contract fit with your business plan or BD strategy?
- Is it core to your business or a wild deviation with a dose of wishful thinking?
  The clearer your target market(s), the easier it is to see if an opportunity fits it or not.

- Have you calculated the opportunity cost of bidding?
  The risk is that you miss out on easier opportunities, or neglect existing clients or programmes because your attention was diverted to the bid.

- Will the client be a breeze or a nightmare to work with?
  If they're known for being demanding or unreliable, with unrealistic expectations of their suppliers, it may be best to leave well alone. Speak to other organizations that have worked with them.

- Do you like them as people?
- Can you see yourself working with them in three, five, seven years?
- Is there rapport and chemistry there, or are you already sensing tension, either in you or them?

Be aware of potential conflicts of interest and other unintended effects of winning. A recruitment agency I know had to turn down a lucrative opportunity because the skillset the buyer sought was almost identical to that of an existing client. And bidding to a tobacco manufacturer or a pharmaceutical company that practises vivisection might create internal tension or moral ambiguity.

- Would winning the contract create any conflicts of interest?
- And might winning it affect staff morale?

Finally…
- In your heart of hearts, how badly do you really want them as a client? Your desire to win is the motive force behind the late nights, the meticulous attention to detail, the readiness to go the extra mile. If you lack desire and you're going through the motions, the client and your team will pick up on that.

DELIVERABILITY
You must be able to deliver the contract to the client's satisfaction. Don't be seduced by short-term gain if your reputation could be damaged by a less than excellent job.
- Your organization may have the right skills, but does it have them in sufficient quantity to deliver?
- Do you have the right geographical coverage?
- If a key team member leaves or goes off sick, does your squad have strength in depth?
- Is your technical expertise current and up to the job? Have you got the right skills?
- Do you have the resources to deliver, especially if the contract is larger than you're used to?
- Are there particular technical, cultural, political or geographical constraints?

Having to bring in special experts to deliver key parts of the contract may complicate delivery and affect your pricing.

PROFITABILITY
- Will it boost or batter the bottom line? Will your gross profit margin be acceptable to you?
- If the contract is in a new market, what are the typical margins?
- Is there repeat business lurking within, justifying a longer game?

- How prescriptive is the contract? Will you have room to move, or will you be cutting corners or clawing back costs through contract variations?
- Will the account take so much time, care and management attention that your ROI will be poor?
- If you're going to have to bid low to win, what's your walk-away price?

A NUMERICAL TAKE ON PRE-QUALIFICATION

The following tool forces you to score different aspects of an opportunity and see clearly if it falls into or outside the 'bid zone'.

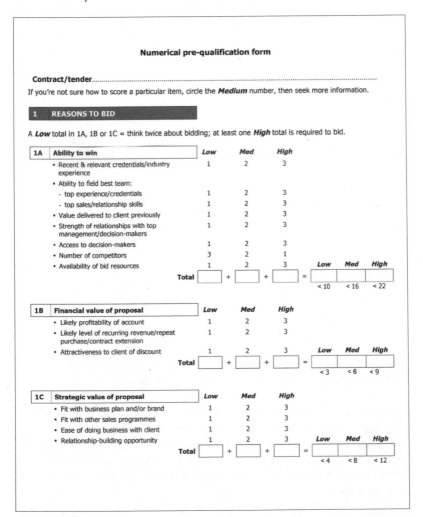

Numerical pre-qualification form

Contract/tender..

If you're not sure how to score a particular item, circle the *Medium* number, then seek more information.

1   REASONS TO BID

A *Low* total in 1A, 1B or 1C = think twice about bidding; at least one *High* total is required to bid.

1A Ability to win	Low	Med	High			
• Recent & relevant credentials/industry experience	1	2	3			
• Ability to field best team:						
- top experience/credentials	1	2	3			
- top sales/relationship skills	1	2	3			
• Value delivered to client previously	1	2	3			
• Strength of relationships with top management/decision-makers	1	2	3			
• Access to decision-makers	1	2	3			
• Number of competitors	3	2	1			
• Availability of bid resources	1	2	3	Low	Med	High
Total ☐ + ☐ + ☐ =				< 10	< 16	< 22

1B Financial value of proposal	Low	Med	High			
• Likely profitability of account	1	2	3			
• Likely level of recurring revenue/repeat purchase/contract extension	1	2	3			
• Attractiveness to client of discount	1	2	3	Low	Med	High
Total ☐ + ☐ + ☐ =				< 3	< 6	< 9

1C Strategic value of proposal	Low	Med	High			
• Fit with business plan and/or brand	1	2	3			
• Fit with other sales programmes	1	2	3			
• Ease of doing business with client	1	2	3			
• Relationship-building opportunity	1	2	3	Low	Med	High
Total ☐ + ☐ + ☐ =				< 4	< 8	< 12

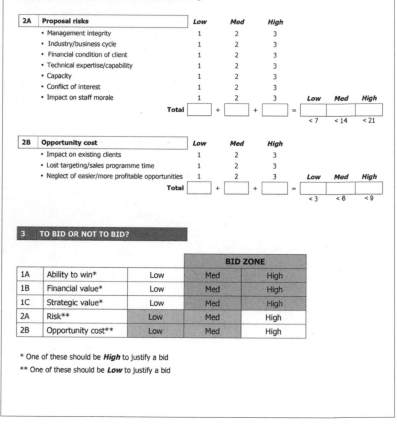

PRE-QUALIFY THE OPPORTUNITY *continued*

2   REASONS NOT TO BID

Note: High total in 2A or 2B = think twice about bidding.

2A	Proposal risks	Low	Med	High
	• Management integrity	1	2	3
	• Industry/business cycle	1	2	3
	• Financial condition of client	1	2	3
	• Technical expertise/capability	1	2	3
	• Capacity	1	2	3
	• Conflict of interest	1	2	3
	• Impact on staff morale	1	2	3

Total [　] + [　] + [　] = [　]　Low < 7　Med < 14　High < 21

2B	Opportunity cost	Low	Med	High
	• Impact on existing clients	1	2	3
	• Lost targeting/sales programme time	1	2	3
	• Neglect of easier/more profitable opportunities	1	2	3

Total [　] + [　] + [　] = [　]　Low < 3　Med < 6　High < 9

3   TO BID OR NOT TO BID?

			BID ZONE	
1A	Ability to win*	Low	Med	High
1B	Financial value*	Low	Med	High
1C	Strategic value*	Low	Med	High
2A	Risk**	Low	Med	High
2B	Opportunity cost**	Low	Med	High

* One of these should be **High** to justify a bid
** One of these should be **Low** to justify a bid

Investigate their payment terms: working for an organization with 90-day terms may impair your cash flow or even bankrupt you.

Whatever conclusion you come to at the end of the pre-qualification meeting – whether to stick or twist, even if you agree to ignore your own numerical score for sound reasons – I want you to be able to say hand on heart that you looked long and hard at the opportunity. Only then will you be able to claim that, if you decide to proceed, you are doing so with your eyes wide open.

STORY:
PITCHING FOR THE FUTURE

Vanessa, a good friend of mine, runs her own wine PR agency. She recently pitched for a three-year contract valued at €500,000 p.a., involving a written document followed by an oral presentation to a panel of 20 committee members. Each member's voting power related to their wine export volumes. It turned out that a couple of panel members wielded much more power than anyone else. They were set on promoting the brand for volume at any cost, whereas Vanessa was clear that they should be building the brand for the future through strategic positioning and creative image building. As a result, she wasn't appointed. But the panel was unanimous that her document and presentation had been head and shoulders above the rest. When I asked Vanessa whether she knew of the committee members' inordinate power before deciding to bid and that she'd probably lose, she said: "Yes, I did. I didn't win that particular contract, but now 20 influential people know about me and my company, so it was worth it!"

Once you've pre-qualified and decided to bid, whoever's in charge of tracking your organization's BD activity needs to post the tender on the sales pipeline. Now you've done your due diligence, that ITT or RFP has become a real tender with immovable deadlines. Posting it to your pipeline should spark the locomotive of your tendering function into life.

If you've followed it properly and you've decided to bid, your pre-qualification process should already have got you thinking about the ideal bid team, which is what the next chapter deals with.

WINNER TAKES ALL
BOTTOM LINE

Every bid you submit – and the process leading up to it – must be nothing short of excellent. One way of doing that is to be choosier about the opportunities you go for through systematic, rigorous and consistent pre-qualification. Everyone in your organization who has anything to do with bids, tenders and proposals must understand that pre-qualifying opportunities is a cornerstone of best practice. This understanding needs to be in your organization's DNA.

FOOD FOR THOUGHT

Let's map your organization's genome.

Score each of the following three statements out of 10, where 1 = totally disagree and 10 = totally agree:

1. Your organization, including its senior managers, has an established understanding, culture and habitual practice of pre-qualifying every major bid, tender or proposal opportunity.	/10
2. Every bid, tender or proposal opportunity gets pre-qualified via a structured, facilitated meeting of all the key stakeholders in the opportunity, against clear Bid/No Bid criteria.	/10
3. Every pre-qualification meeting concludes with a Bid/No Bid decision, or at least a set of actions with clear accountabilities and deadlines (e.g. to get back to the team with more information before taking the decision).	/10
TOTAL:	/30

If your total score out of 30 is 15 or less, it's likely that your organization is not pre-qualifying properly. As a result, you may be bidding for unwinnable or undesirable opportunities. Consider implementing a more rigorous approach to pre-qualifying 'pyrite' opportunities: they glitter in the sunshine of your optimism, but they're not gold.

principle

2

Choose the best team

CHAPTER SUMMARY

1. Why your team selection is vital.
2. What a winning team looks like.
3. How to match your team with the client's by role and personality.

You've decided to go for the bid.

Not only must you select the team, it must be the best possible team. If you merely field the people who are available and not the best, or wheel out the same old team, you're immediately at a disadvantage. Ernst & Young research clearly showed that clients buy the team first, then the firm. People buy from people.

You could argue that Ernst & Young's global reputation would be enough to reassure any buyer, so the firm was never going to be an issue. But in my experience, **whatever the size of the bidding organization, clients judge the team first and the organization second.**

> *"The difference was the strength of the team.*
> *They were very impressive and there*
> *wasn't a point of weakness."*
> A regional manufacturing client

Fielding your best team also differentiates you from the competition and signals to the client that you mean to win.

> *"The fact that their team seemed so right gave*
> *an impression of more commitment."*
> An international construction client

And you must be clear, both to the client and internally, that the team that wins the work will do the work. No 'bait & switch', please, where you field your best, most experienced team to win the tender, then have a junior team turn up to do the work. You don't want a reputation for doing that in your marketplace.

Clearly not every organization is a Big Four accountancy firm or management consulting practice that can pick and choose from a large pool of qualified people. Maybe you're an SME and your choice of personnel is limited. In that case it's even more important that you make the link between a team member's experience and their proposed role on the bid explicit to the client.

WHAT DOES 'THE WINNING TEAM' LOOK LIKE?

Here's my 'get out of jail free' card: the best team is the most attractive one to the client. As every client is different, each bid team should be different, too. The most attractive teams:

1. Are competent, i.e. can do the job
2. Match the client's needs, selection criteria and style
3. Are clear about their roles and responsibilities
4. Demonstrate strong personal qualities
5. Are ones the client has had a hand in choosing
6. Have informed views on the client's business.

Let's look at these in more detail.

1. COMPETENCE

Your ability to do the job ('proficiency') is a given. Most clients will assume you are competent, especially if you've passed the public sector PQQ (pre-qualification questionnaire, Principle 1) and they've invited you to submit a formal response or to present at a pitch. If you doubt your technical ability to deliver against the contract, you shouldn't be bidding. But this won't be an issue if you've pre-qualified properly.

In my experience, many bidders go wrong here: they think that proving their technical competence will carry the day, so they invest most of their energy and resources into that aspect of their response. But that proof is merely the baseline for your bid and the client's expectations. It's essential but not sufficient to win the contract.

What carries the day is showing the client how you will apply that technical competence to their particular issue or need. And that benefits-led demonstration needs to be concrete, specific, detailed and compelling. We cover this in more detail in chapter 4 when we discuss your written submission.

Most clients seek new ideas and approaches, couched under 'added value'. So the people you choose must not only be competent, but also bring something different and special to the table. Examples include legal expertise in intellectual property (IP) for SMEs, experience of horizontal well drilling for oil and gas in extreme formations, or the ability to deliver transformational training in writing skills.

2. MATCH THE CLIENT

The idea of matching, mirroring or level-selling when choosing your team is a principle of rapport-building – we tend to like and follow people who we think are like us. The challenge is to match your team members with their opposite numbers in the client in terms of role, grade and experience. Common sense suggests that the people who will be working closest together on the contract need to get on and see eye to eye both professionally and personally.

We must also match the client's diversity in terms of age, race and gender, especially in the voluntary and community sector. I heard about a company bidding for a contract to audit a regional drug rehabilitation charity. The bidder sent along three white, middle-aged males... only to find that the selection panel comprised two Afro-Caribbean women and a young white male. The mismatch was stark.

Mirroring the client is also about recognizing their psychological needs, such as needing 'comfort'. This is typically provided by fielding a senior person in your team, often referred to as 'the grey hair' or the 'safe pair of hands'. Their 'been-there-done-it-got-the-T-shirt' experience reassures the client that the team is unlikely to be thrown by an issue or obstacle they've never seen before.

You can use this reassurance factor in bids where you're facing a new bidder on the block. If you're up against a young, dynamic start-up that's getting the client's attention, point out to them that youthful energy comes with a price tag – inexperience.

3. ROLES AND RESPONSIBILITIES

These must be crystal-clear, otherwise you'll confuse the client. Here are the four main questions that most clients need answered when they're assessing a bid team:
1. Who's the captain? Who's leading the bid?
2. Whom will I see most of when the contract's running?
3. Who's ultimately accountable for the team's performance?
4. Whom can I go to if things start to go wrong?

In a partnership, such as a law firm or accounting practice, the bid is likely to be led by a partner (1); he or she may well also answer for the team's performance (3). The person delivering the nuts and bolts of the contract, however, will probably be relatively junior, e.g. an Audit Manager in an accountancy practice, or an Associate or Client Services Manager in a law firm (2). And if the client needs to go over the head of the bid leader, then there is usually someone playing a role that I would call 'Client Relationship Manager' who oversees all their firm's dealings with the client's organization (4). This is the professional services firm equivalent of a Key Account Manager.

When clarifying roles and responsibilities, sporting analogies come into their own.

When the England rugby team was thrashed 36-0 by South Africa in the pool stage of the 2007 World Cup in France, everyone wrote them off as the worst defence of a World Cup ever (if you're not into rugby or were on a different planet at the time, England had won the World Cup in 2003). But they went on to beat Australia and France (and lose to the Springboks again in the final). In an article in *The Sunday Times*, Josh Lewsey, a top England player, explained that the team was confused about how they should play. They stopped the rot by clarifying everyone's role:

> As the meeting went on and with everyone coming from different clubs with each of them possessing different game plans, it became clear that there was genuine confusion about how we were trying to play. **We needed a simplified, unified plan and for everyone to understand their roles within it.** The answer was obvious. The decision-makers on the field who played at nine, 10 and 12 should describe what they needed in a clear, concise manner to the players around them.
>
> The following day the decision-makers made a presentation about how they felt the team should play.

FIGURE 2.1. Extract from an interview in *The Sunday Times* with England rugby player Josh Lewsey on the importance of clarifying players' roles.

4. PERSONAL QUALITIES

If you accept that the technical competence of your team or the delivery of a technical service is a given, then what sets your team apart from the competition is their personal qualities. These come in a pick 'n' mix bag of Cs: chemistry, charm, confidence, credibility, consistency, character and communication skills.

> *"In terms of audit policy, there's not going to be a lot of difference between them. It's a personal chemistry thing."*
> A national engineering consultancy client

Chemistry is the ability to strike a rapport with your opposite number quickly and easily; to connect with them. This is a combination of attitude and skill. Both can be learnt. Although some people are better at it than others, it's not innate.

The trick is to focus not on yourself and your needs, but on the other person – in this case, the client. See the world from their perspective, find out what they value, how they want to be treated. In other words, **be buyer-centric, not bidder-centric.**

The skill is to understand one of the secrets of rapport-building: if you (discreetly) mirror their body image with your own, you will find it easier to relate to what they are saying, thinking and feeling. Just make sure you err on the side of mirroring their behaviour rather than mimicking it. People instinctively know if you're making fun of them or being insincere.

Charm is closely related to chemistry. It's about putting the other person first and making them feel as if, there and then, they're the most important person in the world to you. It's a subtle form of flattery.

Confidence comes from several sources, including healthy self-esteem, solid expertise and long experience. You need to approach the bid 'with faith' (the original meaning of 'confidence') that you can solve their problems and address their needs. It's linked to having a 'can-do' attitude that nothing is too much trouble, all problems have a solution and you will do whatever it takes to find it.

Communication skills are too big a subject to cover here in depth, but they include the ability and desire to listen actively and hear the client's underlying message, as well as explain complex technicalities to non-technical people in plain English, without patronizing them. People underestimate the ability to listen to another person non-judgementally, without interference from their own commentary, analysis or self-talk.

Credibility is more to do with how the client perceives you, i.e. your believability. Do they heed your views and opinions? Do people listen when you speak? Clients need to feel convinced within seconds of you opening your mouth that you know what you're talking about. No matter how brilliant your message, if you lack credibility with the recipient, it won't land.

Consistency means that the client knows they're going to get the same level of commitment, quality and delivery from you, whatever the circumstances. Consistency and service predictability breed trust, and trust breeds repeat business.

Character is about the deep-seated values and personal traits that distinguish you and make the client trust you. These include honesty, integrity and transparency. I'm a great believer in always telling the truth, whatever the consequences. If you make a mistake, own up and put it right. I've seen bids where a team member did just that and rectified the error so well that it ended up strengthening his relationship with the client.

There are two personal qualities that, when combined with the Cs above, can transform a team from good to great: desire and enthusiasm.

As in any competitive activity, you have to want to win. Desire is stronger than need: it's the source of your creative energy, your stamina and your readiness to do what it takes to win. A marketing consultant I know called Bernadette says: "Successful people do what unsuccessful people are not prepared to do." If you're not gagging to win, don't bid.

And genuine enthusiasm is a rare quality in business today. Again, it generates energy, not just for the enthusiast but also for the people around them; it infects them. This viral quality makes the enthusiast attractive to us, especially if they're being enthusiastic about our business. As a client once said to me:

> "We want to work with people who want to work with us.
> We're the most important company to us and we want
> them to match that level of enthusiasm."

5. LET THE CLIENT CHOOSE THE TEAM

Provided you have a pool of people to choose from, give the client a hand in the selection of the delivery team. That will make them feel closer to and more engaged in your bid, making it harder for them to reject it. Position it not as your team, but theirs.

And if you can't offer them several candidates for the same position, at least demonstrate how and why they are the best person for the job. So rather than present the client with a standard CV of the candidate, tailor it: make the link between their proposed role on the job and their experience explicit.

6. HAVE AN INFORMED VIEW ON THE CLIENT'S BUSINESS

Another finding of research into bids and tenders is that clients worth their salt value robust views on their business, provided those views are well researched and thought through. I call this 'commercial personality'. Even if the client disagrees with you when you meet them in the pre-submission meetings (next chapter), strong views trigger a conversation that will stimulate them, get them thinking differently about their issues, and make them respect you.

> *"The guy I met was interested in the business. He had ideas,*
> *so you could actually have a discussion with him..."*
> A banking client

The alternative of just going in there to 'fill your information buckets' is a non-starter. That will bore the client and could well dash your bid there and then. By expressing your commercial personality, you're differentiating yourself from the competition.

The bottom line is that, if you think through the client's needs and help them gain new insights into them, you've added value before you've even put pen to paper.

HOW DO YOU CHOOSE THE WINNING TEAM?

You choose the best team not in a vacuum, but as a function of the requirements of the contract and of the client's team. And you need to consider two dimensions of every member of the client team:
- Their role in the buying process
- Their personality.

I often hear the buying organization in a bid referred to as 'the client', as you might expect. That's fine, as long as you don't assume that all the client decision-makers involved in the bid are somehow clones of each other who share the same agenda, concerns and goals. They're not and they don't.

Each member of the buying group or 'decision-making unit' (DMU) is different and you need to treat them as such. To do that, you need to understand the five most common roles in a buying group:

1. The Boss   4. The Expert
2. The Money Person   5. The Guide or The Enforcer.
3. The End-User

Here are the generalized characteristics of each, plus the filter through which they will typically assess your bid:

ROLE	CHARACTERISTICS & MOTIVATION	BID FILTER
The Boss	Most senior decision-maker, aka the MD, CEO or business owner. Concerned with high-level, strategic, organizational outcomes. Less interested in the detail of *how* you do it, more interested in what they *get* when they hire you, i.e. the *results*. Motivated by a mix of personal and corporate goals, e.g. retire early, protect their bonus, be recognized as a success ('make me look good'), see value of stock options rise, boost shareholder value, enter new markets/defend existing ones, protect the organization's reputation or public image.	• Strategic, high-level results or outcomes • Organizational / corporate • Long-term • Personal gain
The Money Person	Usually the Finance Director, this is the budget holder. They have their hand on the purse strings, sign the cheques and have the authority to spend money. They usually work closely with The Boss. Only interested in your product or service from the perspective of cost vs. benefit. Motivated by value for money and getting the best possible deal for their organization.	• ROI (return on investment) • Value for money • The bottom line • Payback period

The End-User	Regularly uses or manages the product/service. Interested in its performance, features, functionality, ease of use and reliability. May be relatively junior in the buying group, but often responsible for developing the tender spec or ITT/RFP. Motivated by what's best for them, their business function and their team.	• Functional, operational • Detail • Often relatively junior
The Expert	The 'techie' or geek. Has deep technical knowledge of the product/service, as well as its competitors and industry trends. Interested in its supply, features, specification, maintenance and applications, including future-proofing. May use jargon. Motivated by how it works rather than what it does for the organization.	• Technical, operational • Detail, features, 'spec'
The Guide/ The Enforcer	Often an external consultant or advisor hired by The Boss, this role is harder to assess and less predictable than the others. Often asks deceptively simple but tough questions. May bring insights from other industries, sectors or cultures. Motivated by the need to add value quickly, make The Boss look good and put bidders through their paces. Typically less interested in long-term relations with bidders; they can afford to be tough with you. If the role is internal, then it's usually filled by Procurement.	• Varies, but usually strategic / organizational (mirroring The Boss's filter) • ROI, value for money • The bidding process • Proposals best practice

These roles are not always clear-cut. Several roles may merge in one person or, in a large organization, several people may share one role, e.g. where they are responsible for different elements of a complex product or service.

As you might expect, the most senior and influential role is The Boss. He or she is typically the MD or CEO of the client organization and carries the most clout. They will often only read the executive summary and base their vote – and their recommendation to their subordinates – on that section alone. So make sure you read Principle 4.5, 'Write a Cracking Executive Summary'.

Many bids mistakenly focus on operational or functional content, to the detriment of the strategic business case or organizational outcomes. Yet this is what The Boss is most interested in. 'If you want my vote, speak my language' applies to each role.

I recently worked with an international oil and gas company. Being full of engineers developing leading-edge technology, that's what they tend to write about in their bids. That's their comfort zone, their preoccupation; that's what they spend their waking hours thinking about.

But their clients' CEOs are more interested in the performance value that technology delivers. They're more interested in what they *get* with the technology than what the technology *does*. The moment you link your price to the value that the technology adds to the client's performance, the higher premium you can charge.

Having said that, don't now focus solely on The Boss and neglect the other four roles. Proposals best practice says that to get the vote of each client decision-maker and win, the bidder must hit the hot buttons of the holders of all five roles.

DECISION-MAKERS' PERSONALITY

After the role of each decision-maker in the buying process, the second dimension we need to consider is their personality.

There are several approaches to identifying different personality types. One of the best known is the Myers-Briggs Type Indicator (MBTI). This is a self-reporting test that identifies a person's likely preferences across four pairs of opposing personality tendencies: introversion/extraversion, sensing/intuitive, thinking/feeling, and judging/perceiving.

This in-depth analysis of personality generates 16 possible personality types, and I don't propose to go into these here. Much has been written online and offline about MBTI and many swear by it. Besides not being an expert in this approach, however, I feel that it's too detailed for the hothouse of a bid, when we need to be able to assess the personality of our client stakeholders quickly and easily. You can't exactly ask each of them to take an MBTI test, can you? I prefer a behaviour model called Relationship Awareness Theory.

Developed in the 1970s by Elias Porter at the Counselling Centre of the University of Chicago under the direction of top psychologist Carl Rogers, the model is based on the belief that all human beings share one motive – to self-actualize, i.e. to fulfil their potential. This means that behaviour must not be viewed as an end in itself, but as a vehicle that moves us to higher self-worth or self-esteem.

Everyone achieves this self-esteem in different ways, which Porter called 'motivational styles'. Our motivational style influences our behaviour choices in all situations. So our behaviour is the result of our predominant motivational style.

Picture a buoy bobbing about on the waves, anchored to the seabed. The buoy is our behaviour, which may change depending on circumstances; the anchor is our motivational style, which is constant.

Porter identified four motivational styles: Carer, Driver, Professional and Adapter.

In brief, Carers are motivated by feelings and relationships; Drivers are motivated by getting things done; Professionals are motivated by meaningful order; Adapters are motivated by being flexible and keeping their options open. The table below includes more detailed characteristics of each style, their upside and downside, and how to get the best out of each.

THE CARER			
CHARACTERISTICS	**UPSIDE**	**DOWNSIDE**	**HOW TO GET THE BEST OUT OF THEM**
A 'people' person more interested in feelings, relationships and team work than action or facts **Listens more to their heart than their head** Puts the welfare of others before themselves **Motivated by fairness, kindness, harmony and empathy** Sensitive to their own and colleagues' emotional needs	**Nurtures team spirit and morale, i.e. acts as team 'glue'** Is supportive, sincere, loyal, easygoing, trusting, caring and compassionate **Makes everyone feel included/ consulted** Good listener **Heart in the right place**	Can be wishy-washy, indecisive, gullible or idealistic **Can be too swayed by their own and others' feelings** Gets stressed easily, may handle pressure badly **May avoid necessary or useful confrontation** May need lots of feedback/praise to be effective	**Talk about feelings, especially their own** Use 'kinaesthetic' language, e.g. 'I can't get a handle on this', 'That feels right to me', 'Let's get to the bottom of this' **Show you care about the team's dynamic** Be empathic with them **Praise them when they do something well**

THE DRIVER			
CHARACTERISTICS	**UPSIDE**	**DOWNSIDE**	**HOW TO GET THE BEST OUT OF THEM**
An action person, a 'mover and shaker' **Motivated by action and results, sometimes at any cost** Sees the big picture, less interested in detail, happy to 'wing it' **Ambitious, self-confident, direct, impatient, high energy, fast-paced, easily bored** In Meredith Belbin's team model, would be The Shaper	**Gets things done (quickly), makes things happen** You know what you get with The Driver **Has a clear vision and the stamina to achieve it** Is assertive, directive, proactive, decisive **Natural leader**	Can be aggressive, bullying, domineering, arrogant, intolerant (doesn't suffer fools, has no time for people who can't keep up) **May ride rough-shod over people's feelings** Short attention span, so may neglect key details **Shoots first and asks questions later**	**Talk about results, outcomes, action, the bigger picture** Show a positive, 'can-do' attitude **Get to the point, don't waffle** Keep up with them... but don't let them bully you!

THE PROFESSIONAL			
CHARACTERISTICS	**UPSIDE**	**DOWNSIDE**	**HOW TO GET THE BEST OUT OF THEM**
Practical, process-driven, methodical, perfectionist, logical, autonomous, reserved and cautious/risk-averse Needs a clear structure to be effective **Motivated by process, rules, facts and figures, detail (the 'small print'), meaningful order** In Meredith Belbin's team model, would be The Completer/ Finisher	Thorough, rigorous, precise, objective, tenacious **Gets the job done: 'If a job's worth doing, it's worth doing well'** Masters the details **Reliable and self-reliant back-office person**	**Can be ham-strung by perfectionism or the need for more data, research or time** May be rigid and struggle to adapt to a dynamic, fast-moving environment **Can be long-winded or nit-picky and lose sight of the big picture** May be perceived as cold, unemotional or mistrustful	**Follow and respect their process** Talk to them about deadlines and details, rather than feelings or relationships **Give them reliable facts and figures to work with**

THE ADAPTER			
CHARACTERISTICS	**UPSIDE**	**DOWNSIDE**	**HOW TO GET THE BEST OUT OF THEM**
Combines the other three styles **Flexible, adaptable, pragmatic, open, collaborative, tolerant, sociable team-worker and mediator** Listens to others' views and seeks consensus **Ready to explore options and alternatives to get the job done**	**Multi-tasker who can balance the demands of people and results** Ready to compromise for the good of the team **Can adapt to shifting, dynamic, demanding environments** Considerate of others' feelings, empathic and compassionate **Works equally well with all three styles**	May be seen as indecisive or wishy-washy, especially by Drivers **Can get exhausted by making themselves too available to others or by putting others' needs before their own** Accommodating several different viewpoints can result in confusion or lack of clarity	**Involve them** Listen to them **Show you are tolerant of and open to the other styles**

You may find that your client's decision-making roles and their motivational styles overlap. For example, many Bosses tend to exhibit symptoms of the Driver style, while Experts or End-Users often conform to the Professional style.

I recommend you create what I call a decision-makers' matrix when you analyse the client pre-submission. Map each person's role in the buying group, their motivational style, their perception of you and your organization, your contact with them (if any), who else in your organization knows them, and any other information that will serve you as a team when you're planning your response to their tender.

Then use your meetings with the client (next chapter) to build on that data and assemble the right team for the client. Your aim here is to match each member of your team with their opposite number in the client in terms of role and personality. Once you've settled on the team's composition, however, don't just file and forget the matrix. This document can keep you and your team on track as you work your way through the tendering process. Treat it as a live document that you build on as you learn more and more about the client and their organization. When you're planning and drafting the bid document and designing the oral presentation (if there is one), you'll find it a useful reminder of all the major issues you need to be addressing.

WHAT'S THE RISK OF NOT DOING THIS PRE-WORK?

If you don't consciously think about the client decision-makers in this systematic way, you're likely to create a proposal that is exactly the kind of proposal you'd like to receive, but that may not resonate with the client. The best proposals reflect the language, style and needs of the client, i.e. they are buyer-centric, not bidder-centric. This is based on a core tenet of rapport-building and empathy: that people tend to most closely identify with and be influenced by people who show they understand them and who they think are most like them.

> ### WINNER TAKES ALL
> ### BOTTOM LINE
>
> To influence the buyers and their decision-making process, you must understand their buying role and motivational style, and talk to them in the right way about the right things at the right time.

FOOD FOR THOUGHT

Working alone or with your bid team colleagues, think about a recent tender you responded to. Identify the buying role and motivational style of each of the decision-makers. In hindsight, did you or your team engage with them throughout the process in a way that they would respond best to?

Score your handling of each decision-maker, then note what you could or should have done differently. Take those insights into your next bid.

When you next hold a bid review/'wash-up' session at the end of a tender, why not run this exercise with your colleagues, to look at the buying role and motivational style of each decision-maker?

Alternatively, if you support proposals in your organization, for example as a business development manager, think about the motivational style of your bid colleagues. How can you modify your behaviour to get the best out of them on your next bid?

principle

Meet the client
pre-submission

Y ou've pre-qualified the opportunity, decided to bid and chosen your likely team. It's all systems go. But don't start writing yet.

First, you've got to fully understand what the client needs and wants, and what they don't want. It's a sad truth that most ITTs/RFPs won't give you that information, at least not in the detail and nuance that you need to tailor your response. In my experience, most ITTs aren't worth the paper they're written on. That's because most of them have been cobbled together by junior staff from past documents and have mushroomed into unwieldy, over-engineered documents that often ask bidders for a ridiculous amount of detail.

A tender is much more than a document; it's a competitive influencing campaign.

Your goal is to positively influence the client's perception of you and your team, so that they vote for you in their selection process. If they don't meet you, you can't influence them. And if you can't influence them, they're unlikely to vote for you, especially if they know and trust another bidder. Trust and rapport here are key: there's a world of difference between having a great track record on paper and the client seeing the whites of your eyes in a face-to-face meeting.

The ideal is to meet them pre-submission.

Even if you're the incumbent and they already know you, my best advice is to treat the opportunity as if you are an external bidder. Of course, you must use your inside knowledge of the client and their business, but this attitude will stop you being complacent about your standing in the bid. And seeing you take the same attitude as an external bidder will impress them no end.

"But what if the documentation discourages contact with the client?" I hear you ask.

Good question. Here's what I suggest:

Ask to clarify some points in the ITT. Most bid documentation gives the name and details of a contact, often referred to as 'the gatekeeper'. Prepare some detailed questions, which they are unlikely to be able to answer, forcing them to refer you upstairs. Your objective here is to talk to a decision-maker, initially over the phone, and then persuade them that meeting you face-to-face will benefit them in the long run.

I've used this tactic successfully in private sector bids. In the sealed process of public sector procurement, however, you have to tread more carefully.

These days much public sector tendering takes place via electronic procurement portals, to ensure a fair, open and transparent process. But portals occasionally fall over or the tender documentation may not answer all your questions. If so – provided the documentation does not explicitly forbid you contacting the buyer – then you have the right to contact them within the clarification period. Your preference should be to call them.

As long as whoever makes the call is articulate, has a good telephone manner and is clear about their questions, then it's another opportunity to connect with the buyer and demonstrate your professionalism. But if the buyer senses you're using the clarification process to get the inside track or to gain an advantage over the other bidders, then you could find your organization labelled as 'chancers' and harm your bid.

Another risk in the public sector clarification process is that you ask a perceptive question that no-one else has thought of... but which the buyer shares with all the other bidders to maintain a 'level playing field'. Of course, not all buyers are equally conscientious. In the case of a telephone conversation, they may not get around to broadcasting your question and their answer to the other bidders – which is another reason for calling them, rather than emailing them.

Clarifying the ITT/RFP is an opportunity to build a relationship with the buyer. Like any communication with the client, it must be planned, prepared for and handled competently.

HOW DO YOU RESPOND IF THE CLIENT ASKS WHY YOU WANT TO MEET THEM?

Your main argument is: the better you understand their needs, their culture and their business in detail, the more relevant your response will be and the easier it will be for them to evaluate it. The more precisely they can assess a submission, the likelier they are to make the right appointment.

If they still push back, tell them that you have a range of ideas for addressing their needs that you'd like to test with them before writing them up in your written response. Entice them with the prospect of free ideas.

The trick is not to talk about your own needs (which is to win the contract), but what's in it for them by meeting you. Motivate them by relating it to how they will benefit.

If their answer is still a flat 'no' to meeting, and they appear diffident even about clarifying your questions over the 'phone, think hard about proceeding. Signs of resistance or holding back at this early stage in the tender usually mean one thing: they've already got a supplier in mind... and it's not you. If they're not prepared to invest the time in getting to know you now, how likely are they to award you the contract at decision time?

WHY DO FEW BIDDERS ASK TO MEET THE CLIENT PRE-SUBMISSION?

There are several reasons, but here are six that spring to mind:
1. They're scared of the client saying 'no' (rejection).
2. They're scared the client will consider it a non-compliant request and disqualify them from the contest.
3. They lack the confidence to ask, perhaps because they haven't thought through all the benefits (see below).
4. Meeting the client is out of their comfort zone: they prefer to stay in their technical ivory tower.
5. It never occurs to them, especially as the ITT/RFP seems to discourage contact with the client.
6. There's not enough time: the bid timetable is too tight.

WHAT ARE THE BENEFITS OF MEETING THE CLIENT DECISION-MAKERS PRE-SUBMISSION?	
Establish whether there's a budget or not	You may laugh, but many bids end in tears because the tender is phoney; there was never a real need in the first place. Many organizations put contracts out to tender to fob sales people off or look busy, find out what else is out there, put price pressure on the incumbent supplier, or pinch new ideas. Before proceeding, make sure there's a budget and they are committed to awarding a contract.
Clarify and 'contextualize' the ITT	Most ITTs are poorly written and rarely tell the whole story. Meeting the client face-to-face helps you uncover the real needs, issues and challenges of each decision-maker, as well as find out what's really driving the tender. You'll also find out what they don't want. And you need to understand the strategic context of the tender. What I mean by that jargon is: how will the tendered contract contribute to the client's ultimate business or organizational objectives?
Uncover their attitude to pricing	If there *is* a budget, they're likely to have a view on how best to spend it. Don't be scared of exploring their attitude to price, but don't do it in a vacuum: always talk about it in relation to the value that they will get at each price point.
Develop your value proposition or service model	I talk about this in more detail later in this chapter, but your value proposition or service model is your overall offering to the client. It includes your proposed approach, team, schedule, benefits (or value to them) and price. It's the guts of your bid. Your meetings with the client are a golden opportunity to involve them in shaping it.
Build rapport, empathy, affinity	Connect with them, personally and professionally. People buy from people, especially people they like and respect. Get to know them. Convince them to do business with you by showing interest in them and their organization, its needs, issues and objectives. The more they invest in you emotionally and professionally, the harder they will find it to reject you. They will extrapolate this experience of meeting you to imagining working with you. **They'll be asking themselves, "Can we work with these people?" The answer needs to be a resounding 'yes'.**

Demonstrate teamwork and enthusiasm	As I've already said, clients buy the team, not the firm. Teamwork sits high on most clients' mental checklist. They often value the softer skills more than the 'hard' technical ones. Technical competence – the ability to do the job – is usually a given. It's the softer, interpersonal skills that separate bidders. The individual qualities (e.g. confidence, charm, credibility and communication skills) we discussed in Principle 2 count for a lot. And **we underestimate *enthusiasm* at our peril.** Genuine interest in their business and the desire to win and do the job superbly will impress them and get you brownie points.
Understand their culture	Pitching to a local authority will be very different from pitching to an advertising agency. Meeting the client will give you a feel for their culture, style and values, including how they want you to communicate with them.
	A law firm I know bid for a contract with a major UK supermarket chain, but they got the culture wrong. Their bid was slick, sophisticated and slightly arrogant. "You came across as more Waitrose than us" was the client's comment. (In the UK, Waitrose is an upmarket chain.)
Find out who has the real power	Sometimes the actual selection process differs from the rulebook. By asking the right questions, you can find out how they plan to make the appointment decision and who wields the most influence in and over the group. Meet them. Influence and position can be two different things.
	Best practice says that you must meet every single decision-maker. Or at least ask to meet them, and be seen to do so. You don't want any noses put out of joint and their owners opposing you. You want every client decision-maker voting for you or putting in a good word about you.
Position yourselves as equal partners	Too many bidders are so pathetically grateful for the opportunity to bid for work that the client perceives them as subservient suppliers. If you win the job and you want your invoices paid on time and your 'phone calls answered, you need to position yourself as an equal partner. These meetings are an opportunity for you to do that, by behaving as your own person, pushing back (politely, of course) if you don't understand or disagree with something the client has said. You need them to respect you, not think you're going to be a pushover.

Open communication channels	Once you feel you've established rapport with them, ask them if they mind giving you feedback on how you're doing during the bid process. If anything goes wrong, no matter how minor, the sooner you know about it, the sooner you can fix it.
	This is also a good time to tee up your post-proposal research: win, lose or draw, ask them if they'd be happy to give you feedback on your performance at the end of the bid process. They're more likely to say 'yes' here than if you spring it on them at the end, when they're focusing more on contract delivery than supplier selection.
Check you've assembled the right team	You will have chosen your core team on paper, but the proof of the pudding is in the meeting. How does each team member get on with their opposite client number? An immediate clash is not a good start, so you might need to consider replacing them and testing the new person with the client. If you can't or won't do that, you've already got a problem.

Except possibly for no. 6, none of these should put you off from meeting the client, especially when you realize the jamboree of benefits on offer. As for no. 2, it would be excessively harsh to disqualify a bidder just for asking to meet the decision-makers. The worst they could say is 'no'.

Convinced yet of the need to meet the client pre-submission?

Let's deal with four vital points of preparation for these meetings: which team members to take; the meeting agenda; the development of your value proposition, service model or outline concept; and your mindset.

WHICH MEMBERS OF YOUR TEAM SHOULD YOU TAKE?

I'm assuming you've already selected your core bid team, as a function of the skills and experience required by the contract, each client decision-maker's buying role and their personality. Now you need to think carefully about which members of your team should meet whom from the client.

The principle is to match your people with their counterpart in terms of role, grade, age and experience. So, to take an example from a typical audit contract, the Audit Manager – who will run the contract day to day – should meet the client's Finance Manager, who will provide much of the audit data and give the auditor access to the right people in the organization.

Equally, if the client CEO or business unit head was attending, you'd probably want to field your bid leader or senior partner. And make sure that the people in both teams who will most likely be working together in delivering the contract meet pre-submission.

If in doubt, ask the client who will be attending from their side and which role and/or grade in your team they would like to meet. Having an advance conversation with them about the agenda and the team members you plan to bring will flush out their expectations of the meeting. That way there are no nasty surprises or awkward moments when you meet the client for the first (and possibly only) time pre-submission.

HOW DO YOU HANDLE THE AGENDA?

When prepping each meeting, you need to agree who in your team will lead on which topics and who will gather what type of information from the client. This ensures that, in the meeting, you don't tread on each other's toes. Everyone needs to be clear about their role.

It's also worth preparing an agenda for each meeting. While you'll undoubtedly have your own, you must check it first with the client before the meeting. Apart from anything else, it's plain good manners. Seek the client's input to and approval of it in advance. And if they're due to meet different suppliers or have several meetings with your organization, add clearly labelled photographs of your people to the agenda. This will help the client remember who you are and whom they've met.

Not only will that differentiate you from the competition but, when it comes to them assessing your bid, they can put a face to a name. (And don't get hung up on judging looks here: this is about easy identification, not Miss World.)

> *"It was clear they were all briefed to the hilt before*
> *they set foot in the place."*
> A local authority client

SHAPING YOUR SERVICE MODEL OR OUTLINE CONCEPT

You've decided who will attend which meetings with the client and agreed an agenda for each meeting. Now you need to develop your thinking around possible solutions to their needs, goals or problems. **Start designing your service model or outline concept. What's your BIG IDEA?**

This is an outline of the approach that you think will work based on your knowledge of the client and their tender documentation; it's the embryo or 'straw man' of your eventual value proposition. Represent it as a picture or diagram that captures the overall shape, structure and configuration of your solution. The client needs to be able to 'get it' in seconds. Your job in the pre-submission meetings is to talk them through it, get their feedback on it and, ideally, involve them in developing it.

What you're doing here is co-developing your solution with the client. Armed with their feedback on it, you then refine it back in the office and articulate it in your written response, to create a key part of your pitch or proposal: the killer page or slide. This is the heart of your value proposition – tailored to and by the client themselves!

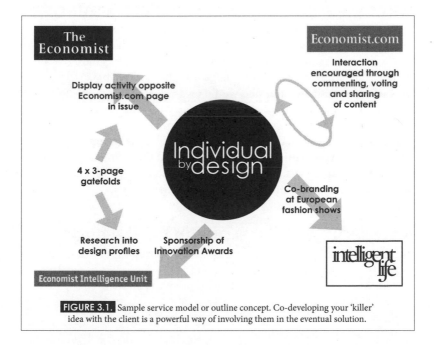

FIGURE 3.1. Sample service model or outline concept. Co-developing your 'killer' idea with the client is a powerful way of involving them in the eventual solution.

Taking a pre-prepared expression of your thinking to the client differentiates you from the competition and gives your meetings with them focus and purpose. It also shows you've done some solid thinking about their business. And if they feel they've contributed to it, it gives them a stake in the eventual solution. They're less likely to reject a 'joint' proposition that they helped develop.

The bid team for *The Economist*, a client since 2004, put together the above graphic to capture on one page their multi-media proposal to a fashion client. It formed the kernel of their written response and the subsequent presentation, and in the Q&A was the major talking point. In other words, it focused everyone on the same thing: the solution. This 'anchored' the team's pitch, as they were able to relate every feature and detail of their value proposition to it.

Can you see the huge value you can add to your bid by holding pre-submission meetings with the client? They allow you to tease out their real needs and issues, nail what is ultimately driving the tender and develop the solution jointly with them.

WHAT'S THE RIGHT MINDSET FOR THESE MEETINGS?

Your mindset in approaching these meetings mustn't be about getting from the client, but about giving to them. While there will clearly be certain pieces of information you want to find out, these meetings are not about 'filling your information buckets', as one junior auditor once said to me. That wouldn't add any value and would be deadly dull for them. You won't win if you bore them.

Remember: **any contact with any client member is an opportunity to influence their perception of you.** If you can get them thinking differently about their needs, goals or challenges and help them see new approaches, you've added real value before even putting pen to paper.

HOW SHOULD YOU PERFORM IN THE MEETINGS?

These all-important meetings are not about presenting to the client, but interacting with them. This is your chance to:

- Test your outline service model and other ideas on them
- Clarify their real needs
- Showcase your expertise (without showing off)
- Enthuse about their business
- Ask intelligent questions and react thoughtfully to the answers
- Show you're a team
- Get to know them and build rapport
- Position yourselves as equal partners.

Literally or metaphorically, you need to roll up your sleeves and show you're serious about delivering what they need.

WHAT'S THE BEST WAY OF FOLLOWING UP AFTER EACH MEETING?

Set the time aside to send them a simple, well-written letter or email that thanks them for their time and openness, clarifies what was discussed and confirms any actions arising. Do this within 24 hours of the meeting.

Finally – provided you have a range of people you can field on the bid – get a senior, non-involved colleague to ring the client and check they are happy with the people they met. This sends the client a clear message that you want to win and are ready to place them and their needs at the heart of your response.

> *"The senior partner rang me and said,*
> *'We've put this team together – are you happy with it?'*
> *I liked that approach very much."*
> A regional law firm

Having refined your service model, it's now time to plan the bid document, then brief everyone who will contribute material to it, especially those who did not attend the client meetings.

PLANNING THE BID DOCUMENT

This should be relatively straightforward.

If the ITT/RFP is prescriptive about the format and structure of your response – which is typical of many public sector tenders – then you must comply with that to the letter. If you don't, you risk submitting a 'non-compliant' bid and being disqualified.

If, however, you have more latitude to submit what I call 'a free-form' bid, then your document can follow this gold-standard structure:
1. Executive summary (for bids longer than about ten pages)
2. Our understanding of your needs/goals/current situation
3. Our proposed solution to meet your needs
4. Why you should appoint us
5. Proposed next steps.

Simple and clear. Feel free to play around with the wording, but not the order. Here's the same structure with more detail:

1. EXECUTIVE SUMMARY
- A brief summary of the major benefits that the client will get if they appoint you
- This is your business case and the most important part of your document (Principle 4.5 is devoted exclusively to writing powerful executive summaries)

2. OUR UNDERSTANDING OF YOUR NEEDS/GOALS /CURRENT SITUATION
- This section acts as the launch pad for your proposed solution
- Articulate and build on what you learnt in your meetings with the client
- Show the client you understand the strategic/organizational objective(s) driving the bid
- Show you also understand each decision-maker's issues/agenda

3. OUR PROPOSED SOLUTION TO MEET THOSE NEEDS
- This is your value proposition or client offering, the guts of your proposal
- Use your service model diagram as the lynchpin or 'killer page'
- Include client benefits/outcomes and link these explicitly to your price
- Include your proposed approach/methodology, the team and their roles, responsibilities and experience, i.e. why their experience makes them perfect for their proposed role on the contract

4. WHY YOU SHOULD APPOINT US
- Your credentials, i.e. you've done this before, got the T-shirt, you won't be fazed by unexpected issues or waste the client's time climbing a steep learning curve
- 'You're a safe pair of hands', especially for risk-averse clients
- Reassure and convince the client through evidence, e.g. case studies, CVs, client references and testimonials, guarantees, warranties, industry awards, statistics

5. PROPOSED NEXT STEPS
- Explain clearly what the client can expect in the days, weeks or months after you are appointed
- Flag up any input you may need from the client in the early days of delivery, so they can organize themselves and their resources

We look at the bid document in more detail in the next chapter (Principle 4, 'Persuade through the written word'). But this simple structure will stand you in good stead for the next step in the process: the kick-off meeting.

GETTING OFF ON THE RIGHT FOOT: THE KICK-OFF MEETING

To recap: you've pre-qualified the opportunity and decided to bid for it. You've posted it on your sales pipeline. You've chosen your dream team and a bid manager to support them. And your core team has had successful meetings with each of the client decision-makers. Now is the time to gather everyone involved in the bid (often referred to as 'the stakeholders') and de-brief them on your meetings with the client and allocate drafting or design responsibilities for the bid document. It's time for the kick-off meeting.

I think of this meeting as a mass briefing session.

This will probably be the first formal meeting of the core bid team and all the other internal stakeholders, and may well be the only time in the process that they all meet in person – especially if the tender is international and involves a number of overseas offices. It's vital that it goes well, as it governs the overall quality of your written submission and sets the tone for the rest of the process. That means it must be thoroughly planned and prepared, a task that usually falls to the bid manager.

If you regularly manage bids for your organization, you'll probably have a number of these meetings under your belt. You'll know that they demand a lot of work. But they're also your opportunity to shine and establish credibility with the bid leader and their team that will stand you in good stead throughout the tender. The investment you make up-front in running a great kick-off meeting will pay dividends down the line.

WHAT'S THE BID MANAGER'S ROLE IN THIS MEETING?

Simple: set it up, run it, write it up.

You need to be clear about the purpose of a kick-off meeting. It's to ensure that every contributor to the bid document has the same understanding of:
- The strategic needs and objectives of the buying organization
- The needs and agenda of each client decision-maker
- The client's selection criteria and decision-making process
- The value proposition/proposed solution that their organization is offering the client
- Their drafting or design responsibilities and associated deadline(s).

Another way of defining the purpose of the meeting is to **use my acronym FFA: Facts, Feelings, Action, i.e. what you want the attendees to know, feel and do:**

FACTS... (what they need to know)	FEELINGS... (what they need to feel)	ACTION... (what they need to do)
...the client's needs, issues and objectives ...the win-themes/ proposed solution **...which parts of the document they must deliver on and by when** ...the client decision-makers and their selection process	**...part of the team** ...valued and valuable **...enthusiastic about the bid and its prospects of winning** ...motivated to devote quality time to their contribution	**...comply with the agreed timetable** ...give early warning of delays or problems in delivering their text or design

Once you're clear about the purpose of the meeting, there's some pre-reading to send to all attendees:
- A copy of the ITT/RFP
- Your summary of the ITT/RFP, including a 'compliance checklist' (a list of the client's requirements, instructions, evaluation criteria and questions that your response must address, grouped into meaningful categories such as strategic, commercial, technical and operational, plus brief comments or explanation)
- Your summary of what your organization knows about the client, e.g. desktop research, press articles and any other information used to pre-qualify the opportunity
- The service model agreed with the client in the pre-submission meetings
- The decision-makers' matrix.

When you invite people to the meeting, make it clear that you expect them to have read these documents beforehand. Otherwise they'll be severely handicapped in the meeting, won't be able to contribute meaningfully and may hamper progress. It's also a discourtesy to their colleagues not to put the work in up-front. The better prepared everyone is when they sit down, the shorter and more efficient the kick-off meeting will be.

Here's a sample agenda, so you can see what it covers:

KICK-OFF MEETING:
SAMPLE AGENDA

THE CLIENT: THE ORGANIZATION AND THE INDIVIDUALS
- Use desktop research/public domain info to build clear picture of the organization
  - What industry they see themselves in
  - Their position/status in that industry
  - The major issues/challenges/pressures they face
- Use decision-makers' matrix to build clear picture of the individual buyers
  - Understand their role in the process (Boss, Money Person, Expert, End-User or Guide?)
  - Understand their personality (Adapter, Driver, Carer or Professional?)
  - Understand their issues, goals, challenges, needs

CLARIFY THE ITT/RFP AND CLIENT REQUIREMENTS
- Use compliance checklist to ensure everyone is clear about the needs/service(s) the client is seeking and what's driving them
  - Are the needs grouped logically?
  - Are there any missing?
- Additional local intelligence, latest industry developments or other client issues

PROPOSED VALUE PROPOSITION/SOLUTION
- Use service model as discussion tool
  - Seek feedback on/input into model
  - Does it need developing, or is it robust as it is?
  - Identify 'win-themes' of your bid
- Costings
  - What are the pricing implications of your proposed solution?
  - Can you deliver it within budget?
  - Do finance/estimators have all the info they need?

DRAFTING AND DESIGNING THE WRITTEN RESPONSE
- Identify who will draft which sections/answer which questions by when
- Brief designer on layout, page grid, front cover, images
- What info/support do authors need to produce first draft?
  - Need to cover for/'backfill' contributors?
- Agree editorial process
  - e.g. Who will review and sign-off which sections, version control, minimum readability score

TIMETABLE
- Agree draft plan, milestones and other key dates up to submission
  - Identify major dependencies and how to deal with them
  - Schedule progress meetings in diaries
  - Get agreement to chase late contributions

SANITY CHECK
- Where are we strong?
- What's our USP?
- What are our weaknesses and how do we handle them?
- What will it take to win this tender?
- What could lose it?

NEXT STEPS
- Bid manager to issue timetable, updated compliance checklist and decision-makers' matrix

From then on, the role of the bid manager is to support, chase, challenge and do whatever else it takes to ensure contributors (sometimes called SMEs, 'Subject Matter Experts') deliver the text on time for the editorial review, sign-off and submission.

WINNER TAKES ALL
BOTTOM LINE

Meeting the client decision-makers pre-submission lays the foundation for success or failure: it clarifies their actual rather than assumed needs, allows you to tailor the document to them, sets the tone of your relationship with them and allows you to brief the wider bid team. All of which primes you for Principle 4, 'Persuade through the written word'.

FOOD FOR THOUGHT

Think back to bids you've submitted in the past three to six months, then answer the questions or complete the tasks on the following pages:

If you didn't already know the client, did you meet them pre-submission?	YES – NO
If not, why not?	
If Yes, rate the value you felt you added to the client in those meetings (e.g. by asking probing questions; getting them thinking differently about their business, goals or needs; making interesting suggestions).	High – Medium – Low
If you scored 'High' or 'Medium', how did you achieve that? Be specific.	
What would you do differently next time?	

Did you co-develop an outline service model / solution with the client in those meetings?	YES – NO
If not, what could you do differently next time to make that happen? Jot down some ideas.	
Did you hold a kick-off meeting to brief all the bid stakeholders on the bid document?	YES – NO
How would you assess the value that the meeting added to the bid?	High – Medium – Low
What could you do differently next time to make the kick-off meeting even more effective? Jot down some ideas.	

principle

4

Persuade
through the
written word

1. The purpose of the bid document.
2. How to include the right content.
3. How to structure and design your bid response.
4. How to use the written word to win.

I n the many years I've spent reviewing and supporting proposals, few have blown me away with their clarity, conciseness and overall impact. Most bid documents are badly written. That's great for me, as it represents a huge market for my writing training programmes. But it's not such good news for clients, buyers or bid evaluators.

WHAT'S THE BID DOCUMENT OR PROPOSAL FOR?

In proposals best practice, the purpose of the document is to capture and build on what you covered in your meetings with the client (see Principle 3) and get you shortlisted for the oral presentation (or 'beauty parade'), if there is one. If there isn't, clearly it's to win the bid by giving the client a solution to their problem in a way and at a price that offers greater value over the lifetime of the contract than any other bidder.

But most bid documents fail for reasons of content, structure or language – and sometimes all three.

INCLUDING THE RIGHT CONTENT

The content or substance of your bid document will depend on the contract you're bidding for and your particular area of expertise. Sadly, I can't help you with that; it's context-specific. However, I can help you with certain types of content that every bid or proposal should contain.

The first principle is to give the buyer the content they ask for in the RFP/ITT, i.e. to comply with their instructions.

Remember when you were at school and your teachers told you in the exam to 'answer the question'? Bids are no different.

When you're responding to a prescriptive RFP or ITT that gives clear instructions on the structure of your response or how to submit it (common in public sector bids), do as they say. An obvious example is the instruction to keep your answers within a specified word limit; if you exceed that limit, you're giving them an easy reason to disqualify you.

Follow their instructions to the letter. They want to make it as easy for themselves as possible to evaluate all the bidders' responses against the selection criteria and reach a decision.

I once audited a submission for a client. They hadn't followed all the response instructions, had skipped some required sections and added others not asked for. Their proposal was non-compliant and promptly disqualified by the buying organization.

As the Head of Procurement at a large local authority once said to me:

> *"Read the question and answer it. If I ask you for evidence of workforce diversity, don't give me three lines and complain when I mark you down for that. Give me chapter and verse, demonstrating your diversity and showing me that you live by that value when you recruit and develop your staff."*

A good tip here is to do what every professional writer does: read the question out loud (ROL).

ROL slows you down by forcing you to say every word, giving your brain time to process and analyse the text. This helps you to understand what the question is driving at and how best to answer it, picking up key words like 'should', 'must' and 'require'.

(ROL is also a great technique for checking your written answers, but I deal with that later in this chapter under editing and checking.)

GETTING CONTENT RIGHT HAS A LOT TO DO WITH MINDSET

Most bid documents are dull.

A number of years ago, I worked with an experienced recruitment consultant. After evaluating over 200 bid documents for clients, Stephen finally threw the towel in, despite the fact that the role was lucrative. Why? He couldn't hack the boredom any more. When he started to lose the will to live by page three of a proposal, he realized enough was enough.

A TV documentary on how scientific grants are awarded concluded that, no matter how academically or scientifically worthy the application was, it had to *excite* the evaluators to win. Serious doesn't have to mean dull.

What makes most bids dull? Answer: they talk more about themselves than the client. The mindset of the author(s) is bidder-centric, not buyer-centric.

WHAT MANY BID WRITERS THINK THE CLIENT IS INTERESTED IN:
1. THE BIDDER'S STATE OF MIND
'We are delighted to be able to respond to your invitation to tender...' or 'We are pleased to submit our response...'

2. STATEMENTS ABOUT THE CLIENT'S INDUSTRY OR ROLE THAT DON'T TELL THEM ANYTHING NEW
'As a finance director, you need to cut costs and deliver shareholder value...' or 'Recent years have witnessed an increase in the use of Lean Process Improvement...'

3. INFORMATION ABOUT THE BIDDING COMPANY
'We were founded in 1915 and have grown organically since then...' or 'We have completely redesigned our website...'

WHAT THE CLIENT IS INTERESTED IN:
1. THEMSELVES
Not understanding the buyer's locus of interest sets you up to fail, by generating problems with content (and structure). Bidder-centric documents tend to:
- Adopt the Super-Smashing-Great school of writing, so everything they do is *unique, exciting, innovative, leading edge, best-of-breed, world-class, unparalleled*
- List the features of their product or service, but don't convert them into benefits for the client
- Delay or bury the client benefits in the verbiage of their document, so the client misses them
- Fail to bring the client benefits alive for the reader with examples, i.e. they tell more than they show.

Weak bids talk more about what they've done and are going to *do* than what the client is going to *get*. If you want to excite the reader, appeal to their self-interest by talking about what they're going to get, i.e. the benefits for them of awarding you the contract.

Here's an example of what I mean, from a law firm's proposal:

CONTENTS

Executive summary	2
Our team and our approach	4
Our project management expertise and resources	8
Our fee proposal	18
Appendix 1: Our supplier service structure	20
Appendix 2: Our value-added services	21
Appendix 3: Our global network	25

No prizes for guessing the mindset of the author. The predominant word in this list of contents is 'Our'.

The writer is clearly more interested in themselves and their own organization than in the client. They are being bidder-centric, not buyer-centric. What would be a better word than 'our'? 'You' or 'your'. But to do that you have to re-write the whole document from the client's perspective. Show them how your product or service will make their life easier, better, richer, or will deliver the objectives and outcomes they want (translate into the language of your particular sector or opportunity). This is all about benefits, as opposed to advantages and features. Benefits are more persuasive than features.

(**NOTE.** When reviewing a bid submission, I always look at the table of contents first. It's like looking at an X-ray of the document: it helps me to see not only the underlying structure of the document, but also the mindset of the author.)

THE POWER OF 'SO WHAT?' (OR, HOW TO CONVERT FEATURES INTO BENEFITS)

If benefits are the way to go, let's first clarify our terms: FAB stands for features, advantages, benefits.

A 'feature' is a characteristic of a product or service. The client may or may not value it.

An 'advantage' is what your product/service does that others don't, i.e. what differentiates it from the competition.

A 'benefit' is how your product/service makes someone's life better in a way that they will value. Examples of benefits include:
- Make money
- Save money/time
- Look good in your boss's eyes
- Get promoted faster
- Live longer
- Sleep like a baby
- Boost shareholder value
- Win more tenders
- Convert more leads into sales
- Get fit
- Be healthy
- Get your dream partner/job/home
- Improve your sex life
- Improve productivity.

Trouble is, many bid writers confuse benefits and features, or simply list features without converting them into client benefits. How do we make that conversion? By challenging them with 'So what?' Here's what I mean:

"Hi. I'm from BabyGates.com and we specialize in child safety products." [FEATURE]
"So what?"

"We're the market leader for child safety [feature]. In fact, we've won more child safety awards than anybody else [ADVANTAGE]*."*
"So what?"

"Well, we've just designed a new, deluxe, 21st century baby gate." [FEATURE]
"So what?"

"It's easy to install with special gate-style mountings and comes in a range of colours to match your home." [FEATURES]
"So what?"

'It comes with a child-proof, tamper-free KiddyGuard.' [FEATURE]
"So what?"

"That means your child will never push the gate over and fall down the stairs." [BENEFIT, FINALLY]

When it feels daft, absurd or negligent to ask 'So what?', chances are you've landed on the end-benefit. This simple little question forces us to drill down from the surface feature to the bedrock benefit.

Now have a go yourself.

Below is a list of features converted into benefits with 'So what?' Notice how there are far more words in the Benefits column than in the Features one. That's a good sign. It shows that we're going to town on the benefits to the client, rather than just listing the features.

I'm sure you've also noticed that **when we talk about features, the predominant words are 'we' and 'our'. Yet when we talk about benefits, the predominant words are 'you' and 'your'.** Another reason to focus on benefits.

The strongest benefits have three qualities: they are concrete (not abstract or woolly), specific (not generic) and definite (not vague). When you add your own examples in the empty boxes in the table below, try to stick to those qualities.

FEATURE	SO WHAT?	BENEFIT
Our firm has 55,000 staff in 20 countries around the world.		You get relevant, practical and current advice on competition law from local people who know the latest regulations and, in some cases, even know the regulators. What that means for you is insight into which of your new products will best satisfy the law in each particular jurisdiction and which ones carry the greatest risks in terms of anti-competitive activity.
Our journal is peer-reviewed.		You can rely on the content, currency and intellectual rigour of every academic paper in our journal. Not only has it been written by an expert in that particular field, it's been reviewed by one. Authors know their work will be peer-reviewed and only published when approved by our review panel. So when you subscribe to BioGenetics Gazette, you get to read papers of the highest quality.

Places on our writing courses are limited to 10.	SO WHAT?	You see faster improvement in your writing skills. With fewer attendees than other courses [advantage], you get more individual attention and coaching from the trainer, who has more time to address your particular writing needs and goals, and give you one-to-one feedback on your writing sample.
		Smaller numbers also mean that you get more opportunities to explore your own writing issues in the group discussions and sub-group exercises. So when you get back to the office, you can apply what you have learnt faster and more effectively to your own work.

WHY ARE BENEFITS MORE POWERFUL THAN FEATURES?

Because **benefits appeal to the client's self-interest.** Clients are less interested in what you do and more interested in what they get when they appoint you and work with you. It's OK to list the features of your product or service, provided you then relate them back to how the client will benefit. As you may have spotted in the table above, a useful phrase for doing that is 'What that means for you is…', then list all the benefits that will get them salivating. Alternatively, use the phrase 'What that allows you to do/ get is…', completing the sentence with benefits.

To sum up, there are three devices for converting features into benefits:
1. 'So what?'
2. 'What that means for you is…'
3. 'Which allows you to…'

HOW TO GROUP BENEFITS MEANINGFULLY

In Principle 2, we identified the five typical buyer roles in most sales situations. Why not match your benefits to these roles?

THE ROLE	THE BENEFITS THEY'RE INTERESTED IN
The Boss	Strategic, organizational, reputational, commercial (e.g. shareholder value, share options), visionary
The Money Person	Financial, ROI, payback, value for money
The End-User	Functionality, operational, performance, e.g. reliability, relevance, ease of use
The Expert	'Techie', e.g. spec, dimensions, product/performance details, modifications, functionality
The Guide	Any of the above

Andy Maslen, my former business partner and co-founder of *Write for Results*, puts it nicely in his excellent book, *Write To Sell, The Ultimate Guide to Great Copywriting:* when communicating with prospects or clients, we need to transmit from Radio WIIFM (What's In It For Me?) rather than Radio WIII (What I'm Interested In). **Transmit on their frequency and you get their attention.**

Remember: benefits persuade and sell; features and advantages don't.

STRONG BIDS ARE NOT JUST TAILORED; THEY'RE PERSONALIZED TO THE CLIENT

We've already established that your buyer is more interested in themselves than in you. To excite them, you must tailor your offering to them; generic bids just don't cut it. But when I say 'client', I don't mean the organization as an abstract concept. I mean the flesh-and-blood decision-makers in that organization, who will evaluate, discuss and score your bid, whom you must get to know as individuals.

We covered this in Principle 3, 'Meet the client pre-submission', but it's worth repeating.

You can't tailor your bid if you don't get to know the client, and you can't get to know them if you don't meet them. That's why either knowing them well already or meeting them pre-submission is vital. Personalizing your bid is about understanding the needs and agenda of each individual decision-maker and addressing those needs in your response.

THE MAGIC WORD(S) AND THE RULE OF 3:1

When we talked earlier about converting features into benefits, I mentioned that when we articulate client benefits we naturally use the words 'you', 'your' and 'yourself'. These are magic words, because they make the reader feel as if we are talking to them as an individual. They satisfy a basic human need to be heard and feel special. Using them liberally is a simple device that is almost impossible to overdo.

And by using these words three times more than 'I', 'we', 'us' or 'our', we force ourselves to talk more about them than us, getting their attention and making them more receptive to our message or argument.

(Grammar geek note: 'you' in this context is the second-person singular, as opposed to the first-person singular, which is 'I'.)

If you have any doubts about the power of this simple word, consider this: if you happened to spot your own name in a bid document or any communication for that matter, would it make you more or less likely to read that document? (See how many times I used the Magic Word then: did it make you feel uncomfortable or strange? It works because it's how we naturally communicate with each other.)

AVOID THE MULTIPLE PERSONALITY DISORDER

When addressing a multiple readership, such as in a bid document, inexperienced writers tend to use 'you' in the plural sense (technically known as the 'second-person plural'). You'll see this a lot in emails, too. They'll use phrases like 'some of you' or 'all of you', as if their readers were huddled around one copy of the document or suffering from a multiple personality disorder.

When you read a document, do you feel like you're part of a market or a crowd reading it? No, of course you don't. You feel like you – a unique, special, distinct person – and you want to be addressed that way. Clients are no different.

AROUSE DESIRE THROUGH STORY

In any sales situation, making your buyer want your product or service is vital. Wants are more powerful motivators than needs. My kids don't need the latest Xbox LIVE game, but believe me, they want it! Ask a woman if they've ever bought a pair of shoes they didn't need, but wanted; most will say 'yes'. Ask a man if they've ever bought a gadget or a tie they didn't need, but wanted; most will say 'yes'. (Please forgive the gender stereotypes.)

Why is desire so much more powerful in changing our behaviour than need? Because when we want something (or someone), desire engages us on a deeper emotional level than need, which tends to be more rational. And this relates to the three principles of persuasion identified 2,300 years ago by Aristotle in Ancient Greece: ethos (character or credibility), logos (reason, logic) and pathos (passion or feeling). Aristotle judged that pathos far outweighed the other two in terms of persuasiveness.

The greatest communicators, from Aristotle and Shakespeare to John F. Kennedy and Martin Luther King, have all agreed on one thing: that **logic makes people think, but emotion makes them *act*.**

So how do we make buyers want to appoint us in a tender?
Tell more stories.

Stories are man's oldest device for informing us, entertaining us and engaging our emotions. They can bring dry information to life through image and imagination, metaphor, drama, surprise, delight. In a bid document, stories take the form of case studies or small examples that demonstrate how your product/service improved a client's business. And in a pitch, telling an anecdote or 'war story' can reinforce a message, demonstrate a brand value or dramatize a benefit. **Good stories make a connection with the audience.**

Trouble is, most case studies are dull and turgid. This is because they don't honour the four classic components of any good story. From the *Epic of Gilgamesh*, carved in cuneiform on clay tablets 4,000 years ago, and *The Bible* to Shakespeare and *War and Peace*, to *Batman* and *Lord of the Rings*, a good story must have:
1. A protagonist (the hero, main character; can be a team or an organization);
2. A predicament (the protagonist faces a challenging situation with an uncertain outcome);
3. Narrative (plot, setting);
4. A resolution (in overcoming their predicament, the protagonist grows as a character).

Here's a simple case study that uses all four story elements:

ALAN'S STORY

Context: Swanswell is a 40-year-old UK charity that helps people who are struggling with substance misuse. It treats over 9,000 people a year and reaches hundreds of thousands online. Alan has been in treatment with Swanswell since 2004. He stopped using illicit substances some time ago but found coming off his methadone prescription a big challenge.

Before using The Swanswell Recovery Model interventions, Alan had tried to reduce his methadone medication gradually. But he suffered many anxieties about doing this, so the reductions were sporadic and slow. This demotivated him and undermined his confidence in his ability to become medication-free.

Using The Swanswell Recovery Model, Alan and his Swanswell keyworker explored different treatment options. Alan examined his anxieties around reducing, and used the interventions in the model to re-state his recovery goals and boost his confidence to achieve them.

A few months later, supported by his misuse keyworker and GP, Alan successfully completed a community detox. To date, he remains illicit drug- and methadone-free, and has exited drug treatment after eight years.

In this short case study, Alan is the protagonist, his predicament is clear and the narrative relates to the support he got from Swanswell, in the form of the charity's recovery model and the Swanswell keyworker allocated to him. The resolution is how these interventions helped him turn his life around.

What's interesting about this case study is that although Alan is the 'hero', he'd be the first to admit that he couldn't have achieved the turnaround without Swanswell. So this mini-story casts both characters – Alan and Swanswell – in a heroic light.

AROUSING DESIRE THROUGH SCARCITY

We can also use the scarcity principle to make people want whatever we've got or to create a sense of urgency in them to get it.

One of the six universal principles of social influence identified by Robert Cialdini, scarcity says that the less available something is, the more people want it. **Rare or unique things hold greater perceived value for us**; we want them more when we learn that they are available in limited quantities or for a limited time.

A petrol shortage is a good example. Supply of a useful resource is restricted and demand typically soars with panic buying; the supply/demand equation loses its equilibrium. In that scenario, a resource that many of us take for granted becomes more precious and we may be prepared to pay over the odds to get it. When normal supply resumes, petrol prices tend to return to their previous level.

Concorde is another example of scarcity, but here the 'resource' was finite. When British Airways decided in February 2003 to ground the iconic plane after the terrible crash in 2000 over Paris, the sale of seats took off. And when its final flight was announced eight months later, thousands of people blocked a major motorway to say goodbye to the aircraft that they could have seen every single day for the previous 30 years.

HOW CAN YOU USE SCARCITY TO SELL YOUR PRODUCT OR SERVICE IN A TENDER?

First, you must convince the buyer of its benefits to them. Then, tell them what is rare, unusual or unique about it. I once read in a proposal: "Expertise in this particular area of competition law is rare… and we have most of it." While that may sound arrogant, they were able to show that it was true, so it became a compelling motivator to the buyer to appoint them.

In a proposal from an oilfield services company offering a new generation of drill technology to an oil and gas client, the author went to town on the benefits of increased rate of penetration, faster production and less 'red money' (written-off costs). But the clincher was in the last paragraph of the proposal:

> *"At the moment there are only five of these drills in the world. Please get back to me by next week to book yours and ensure delivery in time for production on rig XYZ."*

You see, the benefits alone may not be enough to move the buyer to buy. They may still be unsure or scared of acting, so we can use scarcity to counter that inertia. Scarcity can push them to act by inducing a sense of urgency or a fear of missing out on something valuable.

CONVINCE WITH EVIDENCE

Sometimes we need to do even more to push the buyer over the buy-line. They may still need convincing. And the biggest barrier to conviction is their fear of making a mistake – especially in public procurement where they are responsible for spending the public purse wisely.

HOW DO WE REDUCE THEIR FEAR OF MAKING A MISTAKE?

By giving them evidence. We must prove to them that we, our product or our service are as good as we say it is. The most powerful proof is social proof: **we are more likely to do something if we see other people like us doing it too.**

This is where client quotes, references and testimonials come into their own. Of course we are going to say nice things about ourselves or our service, because we want the business. But if someone outside our organization experiences our service first-hand and says great things about it, that's much more convincing.

Strong client testimonials have the following features:
- They are attributed to a named individual (otherwise your reader will think you've made it up)
- They rave about you, rather than being mildly positive
- They are given by someone who works in the same industry, function or type of organization as the reader (i.e. the reader must be able to identify with them).

For instance, if you're bidding for a private sector contract and you include only public sector quotes or testimonials in your bid document, your reader is likely to think or feel, 'You don't understand me, we don't operate in a public sector culture here.' In other words, your testimonials won't carry any weight with the reader and may count against you.

BESIDES TESTIMONIALS, WHAT OTHER EVIDENCE CAN WE USE IN OUR FAVOUR?

A credible track record of delivering similar contracts; statistics; free samples; guarantees; industry awards; positive press coverage; social media 'likes' – these also shore up our claims about our product or service.

Showing a track record of delivering similar contracts successfully in the client's industry sends them strong messages:

- 'We understand the challenges in this type of project, so we can pre-empt them, saving you time, money and hassle'
- 'We won't waste your time (and money) familiarizing ourselves with the terrain'
- 'We already have the expertise we need to handle your contract, so we won't outsource it to untried third-parties'
- 'You won't be paying us to learn about your industry or sector'
- 'Our team is ready to start'.

Stats about the reliability or performance of your product or service – compiled by an independent, credible source – also make your buyer feel surer about you. It means they have more sources to believe than just you.

Giving away free samples sends positive messages to the buyer, too. It shows you have confidence in your product. In the case of a service, you can give value in the form of insights, ideas or other information likely to be useful to them. But be careful what you give away: don't surrender your intellectual property because you're so desperate to win the bid. They may just run off with it and give it to a competitor.

Willingness to do a small assignment for the buyer free of charge during the bid process is another example of evidence, and not unheard of. If you get the chance to do it, grab it with both hands – provided the job won't cost you the earth. It's a golden opportunity to demonstrate your expertise to the buyer. It will also give them insight into what you will be like to work with – a vital factor in their decision.

All of this provision of evidence helps your buyer to believe your claims, which is why another word for evidence is credentials, from the Latin word meaning 'to believe'. They'll be convinced it's safe to buy from you when they believe you.

In sum, we use compelling evidence to help the reader feel that they're not making a career-limiting mistake in hiring you. As the cliché has it, 'No-one got fired for hiring IBM.' By reducing their perceived risk of buying from you, you make their decision easier to justify, both to themselves and their boss.

To summarize this section on content, it's about striking an imbalance between stuff about you and stuff about them. Of course, you have to talk about yourself and your organization or team to an extent, but when you do, always relate it back to what it means for them, the client. Place them fairly and squarely at the centre of your bid. Never lead with your agenda; lead with theirs. Talk more about them than you. Talking more about yourself than them will turn them OFF; hearing how you are going to help them will turn them ON.

Be buyer-centric, not bidder-centric.

HOW TO STRUCTURE AND DESIGN YOUR BID RESPONSE

The structure of any document is simply the order or arrangement of the content, i.e. what comes first, second, third, etc. Design is how that content is presented and laid out on the page. Let's deal with structure first.

Much of the sales communication I come across is structured like this:

EXHIBIT A

Reading left to right, most bid documents or pitches spend the first pages or slides talking about themselves and their organization. They may call it 'introduction', 'scene-setting', 'exposition' or 'contextualization'. I call it 'guff'.

The author mistakenly believes that this is of interest to the client; that it will convince them of the bidder's credentials and encourage them to read on. Trouble is, you're delaying what they're most interested in – the benefits to them of hiring you (remember, they're more interested in themselves than in you). You're relegating your main message to the end of the document in an argumentative climax or burying it somewhere in the middle (the black crosses).

This approach to organizing your ideas is known as deductive logic, i.e. it leads the reader step-by-step through a linear argument or evidence to the conclusion or main message. There are three risks to this approach:

- The reader loses interest and stops reading before they reach your main message
- The reader loses patience if you put too many ideas in the sequence
- The argument may fall over if the reader disagrees with any step in the sequence.

So, invert your structural pyramid to look like this:

EXHIBIT B

Hit the reader as soon as you reasonably can with your main message – that may be the chief benefit of appointing your firm, your major recommendation, a key finding from a study or the main point of your white paper. If in doubt, lead with the client benefits. Put the stuff about you later in the document once you've grabbed and held the reader's attention with what they are most interested in.

This approach to organizing your ideas is known as inductive logic, i.e. it gives the main message first, followed by the evidence, creating pyramids of ideas. This brings three benefits:

- You engage the reader because they get what they're most interested in first
- They save time by getting the answer early, with the option of reviewing the evidence if/when they want to
- Your argument doesn't fall down if the reader disagrees with one of the supporting ideas.

There's a cliché that every document must have a beginning, a middle and an end. What we're doing here is starting with the end. It's the best way I know of making your client communications more engaging.

INVERT YOUR PYRAMID FOR INDIVIDUAL ANSWERS, TOO
Starting with the end also works when you're answering individual questions in a pro forma bid response. Give the evaluator a summary outline of your answer first, then expand on it. There are two reasons for doing this:

1. He/she may be satisfied with your summary and not feel the need to read on;
2. The summary gives them the context to grasp and assess the text that follows, making it easy for them to understand the detail.

WHY DOES THIS APPROACH WORK?

I observe many business writers figuratively 'clearing their throats' before their writing becomes relevant to the reader. In my writing workshops, I often ask the delegate to identify the first thing in their copy likely to interest their reader – and cut everything above that. 'Hack the head off your copy!' I tell them, forcing them to go straight to what will most engage the reader. Cut to the chase. An NHS evaluator in the UK told me recently that if it takes him more than two minutes to find the core of an answer among all the words, he gives up... and marks the client down.

Delegates of mine sometimes push back against the inverted pyramid recommendation. They argue that inverting the pyramid gives the game away at once and steals its own thunder.

I usually respond like this.

In the entertainment media, like fiction, theatre or cinema, it makes sense to lead gently into the story, develop the characters over time, weave the various strands of the plot together and hold the climax back until the end. In narrative fiction, that maintains the suspense and keeps the reader or audience guessing. But a business reader facing a significant investment or purchasing decision is in a very different mindset to when they're reading a novel or watching a movie.

You're not writing fiction here (at least I hope you're not). Your job is to give the client/evaluator as much relevant information as possible for them to be able to make an informed buying decision. In the bid document at least, grand reveals or big surprises are likelier to work against you than for you. And the obvious risk of holding your main message back until the end of your argument is that the reader loses interest and gives up before they get there.

WHAT'S THE BEST STRUCTURE FOR A PROPOSAL?

We see the inverted pyramid working in the classic structure of a tender response. If the ITT you are responding to prescribes the structure, as in most public sector pro forma tenders, you have no choice but to comply; doing otherwise will result in a 'non-compliant' bid and you'll be disqualified. If, however, you can respond free-form (i.e. you have control over the structure), then the five-step structure I shared with you in Principle 3 is a gold standard. Here it is again, with a bit more detail:

1. EXECUTIVE SUMMARY

Optional, but highly recommended for longer documents. The only part of the document that every member of the client evaluation team will read, regardless of grade or role, this must summarize all the reasons to appoint you, i.e. all the benefits the client will get. The client CEO needs to be able to read this in under three minutes. In fact, I consider the 'exec summary' so important I've dedicated a separate mini-chapter to it (Principle 4.5).

2. OUR UNDERSTANDING OF YOUR NEEDS/GOALS/ CURRENT SITUATION

A concise description of the client's major issues, needs or objectives shows that you understand what is driving the tender and how it fits within their wider business strategy. You want the client to say to themselves, 'Yes, these people really get it'. This section is your platform to introducing and expanding on your proposed solution or 'value proposition'.

3. OUR PROPOSED SOLUTION TO MEET YOUR NEEDS

This section is the guts of your proposal. It explains/shows how you will address those issues or needs and includes your proposed team, approach, benefits and price. I'm a firm believer in a killer page that encapsulates your entire value proposition or service model, preferably as a graphic with supporting text (see Principle 3, 'Meet the client pre-submission').

Include profiles of key team members and why they've been chosen for their particular role on the assignment. Don't hide their standard CVs in an appendix in the back of the document: most appendices don't get read. Bring tailored versions up-front into this part of the document. And don't be tempted to tuck the price away at the back of your bid like a mad aunt. Make the link between what the client pays and what they get explicit and clear. Be bold.

4. WHY WE ARE THE RIGHT SUPPLIER FOR YOU

This is a brief presentation of your organization's credentials, e.g. case studies, testimonials, client references, previous similar jobs and outcomes. This is about convincing the client that you are as good as you say you are: you're a safe pair of hands for their precious business. And attribute your testimonials; otherwise the client will think you've made them up!

5. SUGGESTED NEXT STEPS

Show the client – without presuming you've won – that you've thought through what needs doing in the first few days or weeks and that you're ready to hit the ground running. Tell them what they can expect when they start working with you.

Of course, you can play around with the wording of the section titles, incorporating the client's language or terminology as appropriate. But in essence what you're doing with this structure is saying: 'This is our take on your problem; this is how we propose to address it; this is where we've done it before and why you can trust us to do it for you; and this is what you can expect when we start.'

Once again, we're inverting our pyramids at this macro level by front-loading the document with the executive summary (all the benefits the client will get) and our proposed solution for their business or organization. Where we typically talk most about ourselves – in the credentials/'Why us?' section – is relegated towards the end of the document, as it should be.

GIVING YOUR DOCUMENT IMPACT BY DESIGN, NOT ACCIDENT
FORMAT: PORTRAIT OR LANDSCAPE?

When I first joined Ernst & Young, all their proposal documents were in portrait. That was how they'd always been done and no-one saw any reason to change. But one day, maybe because we had a bid that needed an unfolding flowchart that the reader could open out laterally, we decided to go landscape.

It marked a turning point in the fortunes of the National Proposals team and of the firm in general. Clients noticed the change and commented, favourably. Partners also noticed and asked for their documents to be landscape, too. Of course, there's nothing magic about the format, but it did enable us to handle things like graphics in a more visually interesting way. Because landscape allows you to divide the page into a two- or three-column grid, you can lay text out in columns, making it more readable. Most bid documents are text-heavy, so anything you can do to relieve this is a good thing. In MS Word, just insert a two-column table at the top of the page and drop your text into it, then adjust the column widths to create something like this...

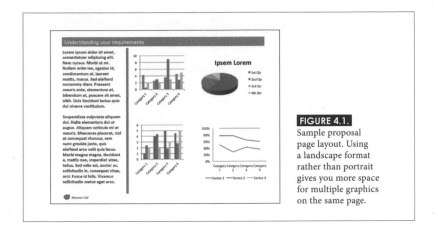

FIGURE 4.1.
Sample proposal page layout. Using a landscape format rather than portrait gives you more space for multiple graphics on the same page.

…or this:

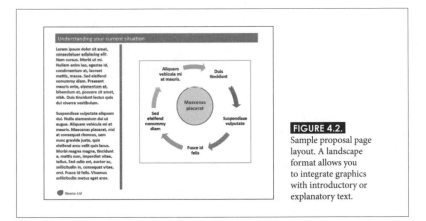

FIGURE 4.2.
Sample proposal page layout. A landscape format allows you to integrate graphics with introductory or explanatory text.

Dividing your page into a two- or three-column grid also shortens the average text width, enabling the eye to take in a line at a time – hence the narrow column width of most newspapers. Long lines of text are hard to read and tiring for the eyes: they trek along the line and then have to make the long journey back to the start of the next line.

The optimum width of text on printed matter is about 70 characters (i.e. about 12 words), and on a computer screen is about 50 characters.

Laying text out in columns makes it highly readable, with three advantages: it's visually interesting for the reader; it complies with the optimum text width mentioned above; and it introduces white space down the middle of the page, which helps things stand out. Try it for key parts of your bid document.

PAGE LAYOUT: ENHANCING THE LOOK AND FEEL OF YOUR DOCUMENT

I'd like to talk about bullet points but, before I do, I must declare an interest. I'm taking my inspiration for this particular section from Jon Moon, whose terrific book *How to make an impact* (FT Prentice Hall) has changed how I look at document and information design. (You can download useful templates free of charge from Jon's site, www.jmoon.co.uk/downloads_ access.cfm; I recommend file 67, report templates you can pick 'n' mix from for your own free-form tender responses.)

Bullet points are over-used.

They were the shiny bright new thing when they were introduced in the mid-1980s, but now everyone uses them everywhere, whether to develop an argument, lay out an analysis, or list recommendations. And there's a growing tendency to bullet whole paragraphs of text, which defeats their purpose.

Bullet points suffer from four shortcomings:
1. They're so over-used they've lost any impact they ever had.
2. They tend to be a random list with no hierarchy or underlying structure, so they're unmemorable.
3. They're hard to refer back to: imagine trying to find a piece of information among a string of bulleted paragraphs.
4. They're visually unappealing.

Jon is scathing about bullets: "Bullet points don't break up dull text; they are dull text."

A quick solution is to turn your bulleted list into a numbered list. If you number the points, you're more likely to think about their order and it's easier to refer to a particular point in a numbered list. The downside is that numbered lists imply a ranking of ideas, which you may not want.

Figure 4.3 is an extract from a report showing the findings of a review of a retail store.

It's dense and uninviting. The story isn't clear. The conclusion comes right at the end, ignoring what we said earlier about inverting our (structural) pyramids. It defeats the purpose of bullet points by bulleting whole paragraphs, with little structure, navigation or clarity. You have to read the detail to get the main messages.

REVIEW OF OUR RETAIL STORE

The finding from a review of our retail store is as follows:

- We got a market research company to survey 100 people in the local area. Two-thirds of people said our products were 'out-of-touch' and 'poor value for money'.
- As for the location, two years ago a large new retail centre opened nearby and is attracting many new shoppers to the town. Unfortunately our store doesn't see them – the new centre is on the other side of the train and bus station from us. We're now in a poor location – footfall through our side of town is down 35%.
- Also, the new retail centre provoked campaigns from local environmental activists. The local Council has bowed to this pressure and designated previously available sites as 'green belt'. There is nowhere else now to develop which means we can't relocate because of planning restrictions:
- Given all this, we recommend that we close our retail store.

FIGURE 4.3. Extract from a report as bullets.

Jon has found a splendid alternative and he's coined it 'words in tables' or WiT. Here's the same text in WiT:

WHY WE SHOULD CLOSE
OUR RETAIL STORE

Summary	First, locals prefer other shops' products. Even if they didn't, we're in a poor location. And because of planning restrictions, we can't relocate. Below are the details.
Locals prefer other shops' products	We got a market research company to survey 100 people in the local area. Two-thirds of people said our products were 'out-of-touch' and 'poor value for money'.

Even if they didn't, we're in a poor location	Two years ago, a large new retail centre opened nearby and is attracting many new shoppers to the town. Unfortunately, our store doesn't see them – the new centre is on the other side of the train and bus station from us. We're now in a poor location. Footfall through our side of town is down 35%.
We can't relocate because of planning restrictions	The new retail centre provoked campaigns from local environmental activists. The local Council has bowed to this pressure and designated previously available sites as 'green belt'. There is nowhere else now to develop.

FIGURE 4.4. Extract from a report, as a WiT.

Now, the main message ('close the store') comes first, followed by the evidence, rather than the bland title 'Review of our retail store'.

The emboldened statements on the left summarize the key messages as a self-contained story, allowing superficial readers to scan them vertically and get the gist. The horizontal rules delineate each point and guide the eye of the reader along to the detail on the right, if that's what they want. So the high-level stuff and the detail are separated, giving the reader a simple choice.

WiT helps the writer, too. Because the left-hand column ring-fences each point, it's easy to see what belongs to each and what doesn't. So it ensures that the author puts the right information in the right place, resulting in a clear, logical document.

The whole thing is visually more interesting and looks more professional.

Essentially, WiT is a table created in Word one row high by two columns wide. You can do it in seconds. In Word 2010, go to 'Insert', 'Table' (downward arrow), select two columns and the number of rows you want, change the column widths to ⅓ : ⅔, remove the side and internal borders, and Bob's your uncle!

Even if you're responding to a pro forma bid, with fields for your answer to each question, provided they are expandable and you don't exceed the word limit, there's nothing to stop you dropping a WiT into the relevant field.

TYPOGRAPHICAL DESIGN: USING FONTS AND TYPEFACES TO MAKE YOUR POINT

Your choice of font and point size is important as it affects the overall readability of the bid document.

There are two categories of typeface: serif and sans serif. A serif is the tail, flare or dash at the end, top or bottom of a character; the best-known serif typeface is Times New Roman. 'Sans' is a French word meaning 'without', so Arial and Helvetica are sans serif typefaces as they lack the serif.

SERIF TYPEFACE e.g. Scott Keyser Proposals	This typeface mimics traditional handwriting and inscriptional lettering, reminiscent of illuminated medieval manuscripts. In the name of my proposals business alongside, you can see the serifs at the top and bottom of the letters S, t, K, y, r, P, p, a and l. Accepted wisdom among typographers and graphic designers is that serif typefaces are best for narrative text and printed matter. The serifs act as a visual railway that guides the eye along the line, making the text more readable. On a screen, serifs are formed by single pixels, which can look like dust. That's why serif typefaces tend not to be used for web or online copy.
SANS SERIF TYPEFACE e.g. Scott Keyser Proposals	Sans serif typefaces (e.g. Arial, Tahoma, Verdana) are best for text that will be scanned or glanced at, like headings and sub-headings, graph or chart labels, road signs, maps and text on a screen. These typefaces are 'monoweight', i.e. the ascenders and descenders of each character are the same size. There are no serifs or squiggly bits, so they are more *legible*. This is especially clear on a screen. Monoweight characters are formed by uniform numbers of pixels, so they look cleaner and sharper – which is why sans serif typefaces are preferred for web or online copy.

Remember that Arial is a typeface or family of fonts, while '**Arial Black 11 point**' is a font.

MIX AND MATCH TYPEFACE – BUT DON'T OVERDO IT

If your continuous text or prose is in Times New Roman, or Minion Pro (like this one), consider putting your headings and sub-headings in a sans serif typeface, such as Arial or Century Gothic (like the sub-heading above).

This creates typographical variety in your document that will help keep your reader's attention.

But don't mix more than two typefaces on a page, unless you've studied design or typography. Too many typefaces can set up a conflict and look to the reader as if it's happened by accident rather than by design.

CONTENTS AND PAGINATION

If your document is of a decent length and you want your client evaluator to be able to find what they need quickly and easily, you must have a list of contents at the front of the document.

Every version of Word allows you to insert a standard table of contents (TOC), where you choose which level of heading to display. I usually go to two sub-levels, but it depends on how much detail you have in your document. As the document changes and grows, you can update the table by right-clicking on it and ticking 'update entire table'. Just make sure that the first line of text beneath a section heading or sub-heading hasn't taken on the style of that heading: if so, that line of text will also show up in the contents list.

Hand in glove with the contents list is the pagination. Make sure that the page numbers in the document footer are clear and not obscured by a copyright symbol or the name / reference no. of the bid. There's nothing more annoying for an evaluator than page numbers and contents that don't match up.

If your bid document is particularly long, with several sections, consider using tabbed dividers in a ring binder system. The advantage of a ring binder is that if different sections are marked by different people, they can be taken out and handled separately.

Use colour, too, but only as a navigational aid: colour-code different sections of the document for easy identification, but not the text. Keep the text the same colour: black. And don't be tempted to play around with livid colour combinations to jazz up your document. They can make it look tacky and overworked.

HOW TO USE THE WRITTEN WORD TO WIN

Most of the hundreds of bid documents I've reviewed in my time suffer from five writing ailments:

1. Wordiness
2. Overly formal language
3. Long sentences
4. Jargon, management-speak and SOWs (severely over-used words)
5. Dull language.

In this particular section, I'm going to share six drafting techniques with you that, if you're not already using them, will improve your bid documents (and most of your other sales communications) overnight.

I can make that bold claim because the techniques are so simple I'm amazed they're not part of the British educational system's National Curriculum. (I've actually identified 21 persuasive writing techniques, but sadly I don't have enough space to go into them all here. I plan to write a book about them shortly, so keep your eyes on Amazon and the book-stands).

DRAFTING TECHNIQUE #1: OMIT NEEDLESS WORDS
Most bid writers want to write concisely – **and most evaluators want to mark concise bid documents.**

The single best way to write concisely is to omit redundant or needless words, i.e. words that don't add any value, content, meaning or information. When we write concisely, we create text that's like a piece of vacuum-sealed food: it's tight, taut and fresh.

Here's a list of 20 needlessly wordy phrases. Have a go at substituting them with one or at the most two words; you'll find the answers at the end of this chapter.

1	for the purpose of	11	due to the fact that
2	for the reason that	12	except in a very few instances
3	in order to	13	in close proximity to
4	in the event that	14	it is often the case that
5	on the grounds that	15	in short supply
6	with reference to	16	involve the necessity of
7	face up to	17	make the acquaintance of
8	assuming that	18	notwithstanding the fact that
9	coming to an end	19	on account of the fact that
10	during the time that	20	subsequent to

At this point in my writing workshop, someone usually pipes up, "Yes, but if you want to impress the reader, surely it helps to use big words?"

I respond to this by asking a question back: "What's the risk in using big words?" The obvious answer is that you might obscure your meaning and lose the reader. And that's not going to impress them one bit.

What *will* most impress your reader?

Cracking content conveyed clearly and simply, such that they get it in one go. That will blow them away, partly because it's rarer than hens' teeth.

The belief that using fancy words will impress your reader and get them to do what you want is A BIG MYTH. Good ideas and great content stand on their own; they don't need puffing up, tarting up or dressing up. And if you need to convey your ideas within a strict word limit where every character is at a premium, then you must write concisely.

I'd like to close Drafting Technique #1 by quoting from a gem of a book on writing, *The Elements of Style*, by William Strunk and EB White:

> *"Vigorous writing is concise. A sentence should contain no unnecessary words, a paragraph no unnecessary sentences, for the same reason that a drawing should have no unnecessary lines and a machine no unnecessary parts."*

It's about economy of language.

DRAFTING TECHNIQUE #2: WRITE PLAIN ENGLISH

An important concept in English is register; a scale of the formality of writing. As you can see in the diagram opposite, the scale has 'Formal' at the top and 'Slang' at the bottom. Let's use 'money', a safe mid-register word, as an example and populate the register with synonyms for it (see Figure 4.5).

In the upper reaches of the register we have words like 'remuneration', 'finance', 'compensation' and 'benefits'; mid-register words like 'cash', 'pay' and 'wages' accompany 'money', while in the depths of the slang world we have words like 'bucks', 'dosh', 'dough' and 'readies', depending on which side of the pond you sit.

What do you notice about the upper-register words?

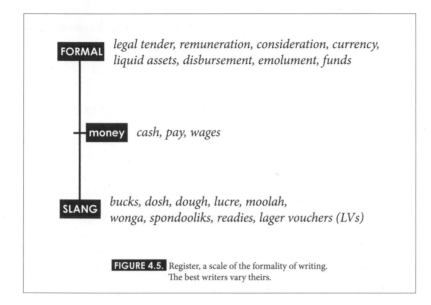

FIGURE 4.5. Register, a scale of the formality of writing.
The best writers vary theirs.

They're longer and harder to spell. They're less well understood. They're more elevated, formal, solemn, distant and aloof. They're more exclusive, so they run the risk of alienating or distancing your reader. If you're trying to sell to me, you need to bring me in close and establish business intimacy with me. Using mid-register language will help me warm to you on a human level. If I feel distant from you, I'll be less receptive to your message.

For instance, which of these two sentences makes you feel closer to me?

We will undertake collaborative in-depth ideas review and enhancement
or
We'll look at the ideas with you and improve them together

I know which style I'd rather read.

Something else very important happens to language as we move up the register. I'll give you a clue: take some money out of your wallet, purse or pocket and play around with it. Touch it, smell it, look at it. If it's a coin, tap it on the table; if it's a note, wave it in the air. Could you do that with any of the upper-register words?

No.

So as we move up the register, language not only becomes longer but also more abstract.

So what?

Abstract language is harder for the human brain to process. In the context of someone marking your bid, it's in your interest to make their job as easy as possible. If you obscure your message with long, abstract words where they have to cudgel their brains to work out your meaning, there's a risk they'll give up and mark you down.

For clarity, directness and immediacy, the best place to be is in the middle of the register. **While upper-register lingo tends to come from Latin and Greek, mid-register is the home of good old Anglo-Saxon.** We call this plain English. So you understand exactly what I mean, here's a short list of upper-register words and their plain English equivalent:

additional	extra
advise	tell
applicant	you
assist	help, aid
beverage	drink
commence	start, begin, launch, kick off
complete	fill in
comply with	keep to
consequently	so
construct	build, make, create
depart	leave
disseminate	spread, share, scatter, give out, distribute
forward	send
in excess of	more than
on receipt	when we/you get
particulars	details
per annum	a year
permit	let, allow
persons	people
personnel	staff, people
prior to	before

purchase	buy
should you wish	if you wish
subsequent to	after, following
terminate	end, close, fire
transmit	send
utilise	use, apply

As you can see, the plain English words on the right are shorter, pithier and universally understood. Everyone knows what cash is and what it does; not everyone knows what remuneration is or even how to spell it – and why should they?

Now, this comes with a caveat: if remuneration is precisely the right term for your technical context – for instance, if you're addressing a company's Remuneration Committee – then that's the word you must use. But if all you mean is, 'You'll get more cash in your pocket at the end of the month', then use the everyday English equivalent.

My message here is that you have a choice: you don't have to use upper-register language all the time for serious documents like bids or tenders. **Vary your register. Great writers like the journalists who write for *The Economist* bounce up and down the register all the time.** They have the intellectual confidence to refer to the UK's immigration policy as 'barmy', Thabo Mbeki as 'prickly' or the future as 'dicey'.

Sometimes they vary the register within a phrase, let alone a sentence or a paragraph. When John McCain ran against Barack Obama in the 2008 US presidential election, *The Economist* published an in-depth profile of McCain where they described him as having 'a blokeish persona'. *Blokeish* is an Anglicism from the slang word 'bloke', meaning laddish or 'one of the boys', while *persona* is an upper-register Latin word meaning 'public face' or 'mask'.

The point about mixing up the register is that it makes your writing more interesting; you can achieve more varied effects than if you stay rooted in one level of formality. It also allows the writer's personality and voice to come through, another property of good writing.

Convinced about the merits of plain English? If not, consider yet another benefit, this time for you as the writer. **Not only is plain English clearer for your reader, it's also quicker and easier** to draft than higher-register language because that's how most people speak.

It's ironic that some writers reach for Roget's Thesaurus every five minutes to move their writing *up* the register, while their reader will reach for the Oxford English Dictionary to bring it back down so they can understand it! Talk about not connecting with your reader.

Here's a final example of plain English, again from *The Economist*. It's the concluding paragraph of an article about Kweku Adoboli, the UBS rogue trader who was jailed in November 2012 for losing the Swiss bank $2.3 billion:

"Take a smart and ambitious person, give him billions to play with, push him to make as much money as he can and do away with adult supervision. The lesson is that this is a recipe for financial disaster."

DRAFTING TECHNIQUE #3: USE POWER WORDS
A 'power word' is a word with emotional kick. Its impact comes from where it lives on the register: the middle.

Because plain English is concrete, everyday language, it's more visual and has more resonance than higher-register lingo.

So you could say:

The Civil Engineering division has reduced its budget for next year.

But if you wanted more impact you could say:

The Civil Engineering division has slashed its budget for next year.

You can't picture a 'reduction' because it's an abstract concept, but you can picture a sword slashing something (or someone) in half.

Take the sentence:

This law will negatively impact on our profits.

Does that have emotional kick? Not really. The phrase 'negatively impact' is ambiguous: it could be a huge impact or a tiny one. It's weasel-wording, hedging-your-bets, sit-on-the-fence, non-committal language (and, by the way, one of a slew of phrases that the British Foreign Office is trying to banish from its communications).

If you wanted to be more measured, you might say:
   This law will hurt / damage / harm our profits.

But if you wanted a greater emotional reaction from your reader, you could say:

   This law will cripple / crucify / wreck / ruin / maim / destroy our profits.

Can you hear and feel the difference? We call these 'power words'. Of course, it's up to you to choose the word that is appropriate, accurate and effective.

DRAFTING TECHNIQUE #4: USE MORE VERBS THAN NOUNS

A serious disease afflicting bids and tenders is 'nounitis': the excessive use of nouns.

First diagnosed by Rupert Morris, a writing doctor, it's infectious and widespread. But it's also curable. The cure? Use more verbs. Here's an example:

   Our specialism is the provision of taxation solutions.

Sounds OK at first blush but, if you identify all the nouns, you'll quickly see it's suffering from acute nounitis. I've underlined the nouns:

   Our <u>specialism</u> is the <u>provision</u> of <u>taxation</u> <u>solutions</u>.

It's bogged down by four abstract nouns, three of which end in -ion, so it sounds repetitive and samey (plus the only verb is 'is'). Remind me, what's a noun? It's a naming word (I often hear 'It's a person, place or thing', which is fine too). The problem with nouns is they just sit there naming stuff, but don't do anything. If the universal cure for nounitis is to use more verbs, what's a verb? It's an action or doing word. So apply the cure to Version 1 and you get:

   We specialize in providing taxation solutions.

That's better, because at least we've got one strong verb in specialize and we've turned 'provision' into a gerund (a verbal noun ending in -ing).

But there's a problem with this version: a big fat SOW is running around. 'Provide'. I'd put good money on the fact that 'provide' (and all its horrible relations) is the single most over-used word in bids and tenders, bar none. Not only that, but it's a major carrier for the nounitis virus.

Whenever you use the word, you have to follow it with a noun, e.g. 'we provide advice', 'we provide support', 'we provide briefings', 'we provide guidance'. Just use the verb, e.g. 'we advise', 'we support', 'we brief', 'we guide'. It will work in most contexts.

So you're banned from using 'provide' in the next and final version. What does that force you to do?

We <u>specialize</u> in <u>solving</u> your taxation problems.

I've underlined the verbs and personalized the sentence by adding *your*. If you object to the word 'problems' in a sales document, you could use alternatives like 'issues', 'needs' or 'challenges'.

So how do you self-diagnose? How do you know if you've got nounitis?

Go through your text and note all the words ending in:
- tion (e.g. facilitation, implementation, collaboration, delegation)
- sion (e.g. conversion, provision, decision)
- ism (e.g. specialism, magnetism)
- ity (e.g. capability, adversity, speciality)
- ment (e.g. management, judgement, assessment)
- ance (e.g. performance, maintenance)

Take your writer's scalpel and lop off those endings to revert to the root verb. You win in two ways: you invigorate your writing, by using more words of action/doing, and you make it briefer, as the verb is always shorter than its noun equivalent.

What's not to like?

DRAFTING TECHNIQUE #5: TURN YOUR PASSIVES INTO ACTIVES
As insidious as nounitis is the passive voice. It's crept into most business writing like a thief in the night. I call it the carbon monoxide of your writing, the silent killer. Most business writers write in the passive voice and they don't even know they're doing it.

To cure your 'passivitis', you first need to understand its inner workings. I often use this example because it's so simple:

The cat sat on the mat.

The 'cat' is obviously the subject or agent of action, 'sat' is the past tense of the verb to sit, and the 'mat' is the object (it's what the sitting is being done to). This gives us a declarative sentence: Subject – verb – object, meaning that the sentence is in the active voice (AV).

The passive version of the same sentence is:

The mat was sat on by the cat.

Now what's the subject? No, not the mat! The mat's still the object, it's what's being sat on, isn't it? So the passive version goes object – verb – subject, i.e. the subject and the object have switched places. The sentence has also acquired additional words, like 'was' and 'by', which you need to form the passive. We describe this sentence as being in the passive voice (PV).

What obvious difference between the two versions do you notice?

Yup, the passive version is longer, 33% longer in fact (eight words vs. six is an increase of 33%). And is there any difference in meaning? None. So if you're a fan of the passive voice, your writing will be a third longer than it needs to be with no added value, content, meaning or information. And that's a big deal if you're working within a strict word or character limit when responding to an ITT or RFP.

How else do the two versions differ?

Well, the passive one is less direct, more complicated and makes your reader's brain work harder to decode its meaning. In the context of one simple sentence like this one, you may think this is all a storm in a teacup, but over a 30- or 40-page document cumulatively it will make a big difference.

I'm advocating that you use the active voice much more than the passive. The active voice is briefer and forces you to state who is doing what to whom. Simple, clear, direct.

However, there are four occasions when it's OK to use the passive:

1. To cover your backside.
The passive voice lets you drop the subject, e.g. 'The mat was sat on' is grammatically correct, but we no longer know who did the sitting. So use the passive if you want to hide responsibility for something, or be less confrontational. For instance, you often hear government representatives after

a disaster or scandal using language like 'Mistakes were made, targets were missed but lessons will be learnt'. Classic butt-covering language courtesy of the passive voice.

2. To emphasize the object.
As the passive forces you to put the object at the front of the sentence, this automatically emphasizes it. Based on the theory of primacy, the first word or idea in a sentence gets the reader's attention. So we might say 'The hand-crafted, velvet-tufted 13th-century Baluchistan rug was sat on by the cat'.

3. When the subject is unknown.
Use the passive if you don't know who or what the subject is, e.g.:

'It is alleged that a murder took place' (you don't know who made the allegation)

'A shot was fired' (you don't know who the shooter was)

'Our friends were burgled last night' (they don't know who burgled them).

4. When the subject is unimportant.
'The file was uploaded to the server' and 'The meeting was convened for Tuesday' are classic examples of the subject not mattering. It's immaterial who or what uploaded the file; it was probably an automatic process anyway. And does it matter who convened the meeting? These are two examples where the action is more important than the actor.

A word of warning on the passive voice: people sometimes confuse voice with tense, but they're two different things. The voice of a sentence is binary: it's either active or passive. A tense, however, locates an action in time, e.g. 'We are being offered a discount' is in both the present tense and the passive voice; 'we were offered a discount' is in the past tense and the passive; 'we will be offered a discount' is in the future tense and the passive.

Sorry if you already know this, but some people think you can't change tenses in the passive; you can. So, to revert to our original example, you can just as easily say:

The mat is being sat on by the cat (present tense + PV)
as
The mat will be sat on by the cat (future tense + PV)
as

The mat would be sat on by the cat, if the cat was in the room
(conditional tense + PV).

My take-away message, though, is this: **if you want your writing to be briefer, more direct and more dynamic, make the active voice your voice of choice.**

DRAFTING TECHNIQUE #6: SHOW, DON'T TELL

There's a widespread tendency in sales documents to tell the client what you're good at but not demonstrate it. This generates what I call the Super-Smashing-Great school of writing:

We are committed to providing you with unique, exciting, best-of-breed, state-of-the-art, cutting-edge, market-leading IT solutions that will transform the productivity of your sales force and streamline your sales process.

This horrible sentence is awash with generic, boastful, cliché-ridden but unsubstantiated claims with a high BS-quotient that will send the evaluator running for the hills.

Anybody can make claims like this, but as Rod Tidwell (played by Cuba Gooding, Jr.) says, in the Tom Cruise movie *Jerry Maguire*, "Show me the money!" To be credible and get a good client score, you must do more showing than telling. This is what I mean:

If you appoint us, you will get access to generation 4.5 of our 'Window to Win' proprietary consultative selling CRM (Customer Relationship Management) system.

Developed in partnership with NASA specifically for the management consulting industry, 'Window to Win' allows you to track every single contact with every sales lead, prospect or customer on any device you want, whether laptop, PC, mobile phone or even your television.

The system guides you and your sales people step-by-step through the sales process to:
- *Target an industry sector or niche*
- *Pre-qualify 'suspects' into prospects*
- *Get their attention in innovative ways*
- *Build rapport with them quickly*
- *Prove to them the value of doing business with you*

- *Convert them into customers*
- *Increase the number of times they buy from you*
- *Boost the average value of each sale*
- *Bill them*
- *Track their contribution to your sales targets and your sales team's ROI*
- *Keep in touch with them throughout the life of your relationship.*

What's different about 'Window to Win' is that wherever you are in the sales process, the system prompts you with suggestions for how to move the lead on to the next stage. Based on proven consultative selling techniques, these suggestions mean that you are never at a loss for how to progress a prospect. The system also reminds you when you've let a lead lapse or haven't been in touch with a customer for a certain period of time. It also contains a matrix for tracking the quality of your relationship with the lead and other relevant stakeholders.

The results speak for themselves. 98%* of management consultancies who have licensed 'Window to Win' have seen their sales grow by at least 45% in 18 months, while 97%** say they would strongly recommend it (but not to their competitors!)

* Independent research conducted with a sample of 56 clients in June 2012
** Focus groups held among 38 clients in November 2012

"Despite the fact that 'Window to Win' is the most expensive CRM on the market, it's already paid for itself three times over. We are winning work that before we wouldn't even have looked at. It's put rocket fuel in our sales – and our sales people!"
Joe Bloggs, Sales & Marketing Director, Widgets Inc.

OK, I know I went a bit over the top there, but you get the idea.

Though my version is fanciful, it's crammed full of specific, concrete and definite features and benefits, with compelling third-party evidence in the form of market stats and a client testimonial.

Of course, it's much longer than the original sentence, but that's because I've drilled down through several layers from the surface. Now it gives the reader much more information to base their decision on. You'll find that when you start showing not telling and going to town on the benefits, you'll use more words. And you'll avoid the management-speak, buzz-words and MBA-itis that puts most clients off.

HOW TO EDIT AND CHECK YOUR BID DOCUMENT
You've produced your first draft but you're not going to send it, are you?

Professional writers never send their first draft, because it's usually half-baked and hasn't enjoyed the sculpting, re-drafting and polishing it needs. If you have to send your first draft because you've run out of time and the tender deadline approaches, something's gone seriously wrong with your process.

So pull out your editor's red pen and let's go.

Whether you're editing an entire bid document or a single answer, you'd be well advised to ask (and answer) the following questions, in this order:

1. Is it fit for purpose?
Is your text broadly doing the job you need it to do? Will it make the reader do what you want them to do? Does it answer the question?

2. Does it tackle the right issues in the right order?
If you're answering a specific question in a pro forma bid, your text must answer the question as directly and immediately as possible. If the question asks for several things in a certain order, it's usually a good idea to reflect that in your answer, provided the order is logical.

If you do decide to deviate from the order in which the client posed the question(s), explain why.

3. Is it clear and concise?
Your reader/evaluator must 'get it' in one go and not have to re-read it to understand what you mean. So use simple but not simplistic language; make it easy for them. Would someone not involved in the bid be able to understand it? Clarity is vital, so plain English is usually the way to go.

4. Does it speak to the reader in language they will understand and respond to?
Plain English and appropriate technical jargon can co-exist in a bid. If your reader is highly technical, then liberally use the jargon they will understand (and may expect). If your content is highly technical, then offset it with simpler supporting language.

If there is a chance, however, that other readers may be non-technical, then go easy on the jargon. If you must use it, perhaps clarify it or spell it out.

You might consider including a glossary of terms in your document. This makes clarification available to readers who need it, while avoiding the risk of patronizing them by explaining too much in the text.

5. Is it attractively laid out?

As you cast your eye over the document, is every page easy on the eye? Is it breathable, with lots of white space? Is it visually interesting, using graphics like charts, tables, photos, diagrams and flashes well? Or are all the pages so similar that they merge into one, with little contrast or differentiation?

The section on document and information design earlier in this chapter has plenty of ideas for improving the 'look and feel' of your document. I'm a great believer in making any communication an enjoyable experience for the reader, so also consider elements of your document like paper stock (i.e. quality and weight of paper), a properly designed cover, and clear headers and footers.

HOW MANY DRAFTS SHOULD YOU DO?

There's no magic rule, but the bare minimum is three:

Draft 1: Likely to be half-baked, with typos.
Draft 2: Spell-checked.
Draft 3: Printed out and proofread.

As you can see, that's pretty sparse. No omission of needless words, no pruning of structure or style, no attempt to modulate tone of voice. So if you can, go to five drafts:

Draft 1: Half-baked initial attempt.
Draft 2: Broad assessment against your objective.
Draft 3: Check structure, flow, big picture stuff. Does it hang together, does its architecture make sense and/or reflect what the ITT or RFP asked for? Survey the list of contents for a quick and easy way of checking this.
Draft 4: Review for style, word choice, tone of voice, punctuation.
Draft 5: Spell-check it, print it out and proofread for typos.

Here are the tools you should use on your drafts, in this order:

Deforest your text with a hefty chainsaw, taking out whole sections and pages. Then use the **garden secateurs** to trim paragraphs and sentences. Finally, excise individual words and phrases with a **surgeon's scalpel.**

Too often I see writers pruning the leafy treetops when they should be attacking the trunk, and vice versa.

I'd like to spend a few more lines on drafts 4 and 5.

ROL AND THE READABILITY STATS

At Draft 4, there are two useful ways of checking the style and language of your text. The first is a highly technical device, derived originally from sub-atomic physics and quantum mechanics (only joking). It's called 'read it out loud', or ROL, and every professional writer does it.

I mentioned this earlier in the chapter, but it bears repetition.

ROL slows you down and allows you to hear how your text will sound to the reader. After all, we don't read tone of voice, we hear it. But ROL also catches the clumsy phrase and the sentence that runs on and on (when you start to get breathless). When we read our own text to ourselves or scan it, our brains tend to go on auto-pilot and insert what we want to be there or think is there, but which actually isn't. ROL stops that in its tracks. It's such a simple technique, there's no excuse for not doing it. (If you work in an open-plan office and worry about disturbing your colleagues – or making them worry about your sanity – find an empty meeting room or go for a walk in the park.)

The second technique, coming to a screen near you, is more technical than ROL, but even easier. It entails running the readability statistics available in every version of Word. This is what they look like:

Readability Statistics	? ×
Counts	
Words	766
Characters	3399
Paragraphs	38
Sentences	60
Averages	
Sentences per Paragraph	3.0
Words per Sentence	10.8
Characters per Word	4.1
Readability	
Passive Sentences	5%
Flesch Reading Ease	75.6
Flesch-Kincaid Grade Level	5.4

FIGURE 4.6. The Readability Statistics, available in all word processing applications. The stats give you feedback on key ratios in your text.

Based on the work of Dr Rudolf Flesch, a Viennese psychologist who fled Nazism in the 1930s and settled in New York, the stats allow you to score the readability of your own writing – and other people's, provided you have an electronic copy (I've seen this spawn some healthy interdepartmental competition).

Dr Flesch combined two measures of readability: the average number of words per sentence and the average number of syllables per word. He threw both into a Kenwood blender, switched it on and the algorithm it spat out is what runs the stats.

The stats give you lots of useful data, but I'd like you to focus on four numbers:
1. In the middle section ('Averages'), **your average number of words per sentence should be 15-20;**
2. In the lower section ('Readability'), **the proportion of sentences in the passive voice should be as close to 0% as possible;**
3. In the same section, your **Flesch Reading Ease (FRE) score should be at least 45%;**
4. The final ratio (Flesch-Kincaid Grade Level) is the functional reading age as measured by the US grade school system.

First, **average sentence length (ASL)** is a major determinant of readability. Too many bids and funding applications subject their evaluators to sentences that recall James Joyce or Jane Austen. Long sentences contain more ideas and demand more processing power than short ones. Why make your reader work harder than necessary to get your meaning and/ or score your answer?

Second, as we've already established, passivitis is as chronic an affliction in business writing as nounitis. Writing in the passive voice is longer, less direct and less vigorous than the active voice, which forces you to state who is doing what to whom, so keep your PV to a minimum. The clue's in the name.

Third, the FRE score is a percentage, so the higher the better. In Dr Flesch's system, plain English starts at 60% FRE. Few of us writing technical bids or funding applications reach those dizzy heights, largely because technical jargon tends to be polysyllabic and that depresses readability. But we should be able to score 45-50% FRE by offsetting techie text with simple supporting language (your executive summaries should be even more readable than that, however). **Just because your topic is technical doesn't mean you have to complicate your writing. In fact, you should do the opposite.**

Fourth, the **Flesch-Kincaid Grade Level** measures the minimum amount of American education required to understand a piece of writing. Add five to convert the ratio into age, i.e. a grade level of 5.4 is an American ten-year-old. Many of my clients set a Flesch-Kincaid Grade Level for their external communications of 10 or 11, depending on their readership. It doesn't mean they're targeting that age group, but it helps their writers to pitch their text at an appropriate level of complexity.

If the Readability Stats are new to you, I want you to enthuse about them, but don't get carried away! If a particular section of your bid document demands lots of technical language, that will depress your FRE. Don't feel bad about that. I don't want the tail of the readability stats to wag the dog. It's much more important that you submit a technically correct answer to the client that scores higher on their evaluation criteria but slightly lower on readability than vice versa. At the end of the day, it's only a tool, albeit a useful one.

How to access the Readability Stats in MS Word 2016

1. To activate the stats: launch Word and click on 'File' in the toolbar, 'Options' in the left-hand column, then on 'Proofing'. The dialogue box that appears looks like this:

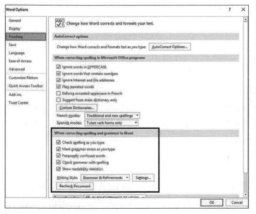

Tick the 'Show readability statistics' option towards the bottom of the screen. Directly beneath that, in the 'Writing Style' field there's a drop-down box: select 'Grammar & Refinements' and, if you wish, click on the 'Settings…' option to further refine what the stats look at. Click 'OK' to activate the stats.

2. To score the readability of your text, put the cursor at the start of the document's body copy or highlight the text you want to score. Then run the normal Spelling & Grammar check (under 'Review' in the toolbar), accepting or rejecting the options as you wish (click on 'Ignore all' to get through them quickly). At the end of the S & G check, a dialogue box asks if you wish to check the remainder of the document. Click 'No' and the Readability Stats appear.

NB. The stats work best on fully punctuated body copy of at least 200 words; they don't work well on headlines, sub-headings and bullet points. If your document has lots of these, save it as a text-only file and run the stats on that for a truer score.

The stats introduce objectivity into what can be a subjective and sensitive area, especially if your boss fancies themselves as a wordsmith and liberally red-pens your work. They're also useful if you have to give feedback on other people's work, because they give you hard evidence of what's going on in their writing.

To close this section, if you score your writing and you get an FRE less than 45%, there are five things you can do to boost your readability:
1. Simplify your language by using plain English
2. Turn your passive sentences into active ones
3. Shorten your sentences to an ASL of 15-20 words
4. Use more verbs than nouns
5. Keep technical jargon to a minimum.

PROOFREADING DRAFT 5
When I ask delegates on my training courses to rate out of 10 the importance of issuing a document without a 'typo' (a typographical error, like a misspelled word), they usually say 9, 10 or even 11. After all, if you can't be bothered or don't have the time to proofread your written submission, what does that tell the client about your attitude or process?

I once heard a great analogy for describing the effect on the reader of a typo. Good writing is like looking through a clear window: you're not aware of the glass, only the view. A typo acts as a smudge on the window. Here's a professional proofreading technique that will banish typos to the past:

Print out your document (it's inefficient and tiring to proofread on screen). Go to the last word on the last page and read backwards, from right to left and bottom to top, revealing each preceding line with a piece of card as you work from the back of the document to the front.

This technique destroys the brain's ability to make sense of what you're reading, forcing you to consider one word at a time. It assumes that you've already checked the sense and overall meaning of the document, as discussed in the five drafts earlier in this chapter. It catches things that spell-check misses, like *sing* when you meant *sign*, and *form* when you meant *from*, because you have enough context from the rest of the line to know which it should be. It also helps you spot double spaces and duplicated punctuation marks.

Most people don't proofread properly. They think that scanning or skimming over their text is enough, but the risk is that they will read what they want to read, rather than what is actually there. This proofreading technique makes that impossible.

> ### WINNER TAKES ALL
> ### BOTTOM LINE
>
> Sorry if this has been a long chapter, but I hope you've found it useful. Let's summarize it with one key learning point: the content, structure and language of winning bid documents must be buyer-centric, not bidder-centric. It's all about them, not you.

FOOD FOR THOUGHT

How buyer-centric is your proposal? Three ways to measure this:

1. Look at the contents list and count the number of times the words 'you/your' occur vs. 'our/us'. If there are more 'our/us' than 'you/your', you're probably talking too much about your organization and too little about the client. You know which way round it should be.

2. Compare your contents list/table of contents to the recommended document structure earlier in this chapter: how close is it? If your proposal starts with who you are, what you do and what's so great about you, you haven't inverted your structural pyramid. The risk is, you'll lose your reader before they reach the juicy stuff about what they're going to get if they appoint you.

3. Open your latest proposal in Word and do two searches (Ctrl + F): one for the client's name, the other for the name of your organization. Count the number of times each one occurs in the text and compare the two numbers: if your organization's name appears more than the client's, chances are your proposal is not buyer-centric.

The gold standard is this: your bid document should mention the client at least three times as often as your own organization. Playing to their self-interest will hold their attention and win you more business.

OMIT NEEDLESS WORDS QUIZ: ANSWERS

1	for the purpose of	to, for
2	for the reason that	because, as, since, due to, thanks to, for
3	in order to	to
4	in the event that	if, when, should, in case
5	on the grounds that	based on, due to, thanks to, given
6	with reference to	about
7	face up to	face, confront, address, accept, admit, realize, recognize, acknowledge, tackle, deal with
8	assuming that	assuming, if
9	coming to an end	ending, concluding, finishing, finally, in sum
10	during the time that	when, while
11	due to the fact that	because, due to, thanks to
12	except in a very few instances	usually, normally, mostly, generally, typically
13	in close proximity to	near to, close to
14	it is often the case that	often, frequently
15	in short supply	rare, scarce, sparse, limited, uncommon, meagre (uncountable stuff, e.g. talent); few (countable things, e.g. skills)
16	involve the necessity of	require, need, entail, involve, demand, call for, necessitate, merit, warrant, mandate
17	make the acquaintance of	meet
18	notwithstanding the fact that	despite, although, even though
19	on account of the fact that	because, as, since, due to, thanks to
20	subsequent to	after, following

How did you get on? Now that you know how to write concisely, you're ready to tackle the executive summary...

principle

4.5

Write a cracking executive summary

CHAPTER SUMMARY

1. What an executive summary is for and not for.
2. What it should include.
3. How to write it.
4. When to write it and how long it should be.

I've dedicated a separate section of Principle 4 to the executive summary, because it's the most important part of your proposal. It's the only part that everyone buy-side reads. It may be the only part that some decision-makers read, especially the most senior ones. I've known a CEO vote for a supplier based on the executive summary alone.

WHAT'S A PROPOSAL EXECUTIVE SUMMARY FOR?

To answer the client's question, 'What's in it for me?' (WIIFM).

Your exec summary should capture the major benefits the client gets when they appoint you, ideally in the three minutes a busy chief exec will give you to persuade them to vote for you. It's not about what you're going to *do* so much as what the client *gets*.

'Executive summary' is a bit of a misnomer: it's not so much a summary of your whole proposal as the business case for appointing you. **The exec summary has no other purpose in life than to sell your proposal.** It captures the essence of your value proposition and primes the reader for the detail contained in the body of the document.

In fact, it's so important that if the tender documentation doesn't explicitly ask for an executive summary (often the case in public sector tenders), you must create one. Find an appropriate place in your response to summarize the benefits to the buyer of appointing you. Open questions along the lines of 'Please describe the value that your organization can add to the contract', 'Outline your overall approach to delivering this contract', or 'What do you believe sets you apart from the other bidders?' are begging to be addressed in this way.

WHAT'S A PROPOSAL EXECUTIVE SUMMARY *NOT* FOR?

Anything else. The exec summary is not there to:

- Introduce your bid: do that in the covering letter
- Tell the client how delighted or proud you are to be bidding: they're not interested in your state of mind or how you feel about the bid, so avoid grovelling phrases like 'Thank you for the opportunity to bid…'
- Describe in detail how you plan to do the job: the client might just pass that 'blueprint' to their mate to do it cheaper.

WHAT SHOULD A PROPOSAL EXECUTIVE SUMMARY INCLUDE?

Break it down into four distinct elements that reflect the body of the document, but with the emphasis firmly not on what you're going to do, but on what the client gets:

1. A brief re-statement of the client's objectives. This should be non-controversial stuff confirmed in your pre-submission meetings: you want the client nodding here.
2. Your proposed solution in outline, including your approach, team, benefits and price (your 'value proposition'):
   - Show how you'll help deliver the client's objectives
   - Make the link between your solution and those objectives explicit
   - List the major benefits of your solution, in terms of cost, quality and/ or time
   - Link the price explicitly to the benefits that the client will get when they appoint you
3. Why you are the right person, team or organization to do the job. You have the best people with the right approach/tools and the most relevant experience. You're 'a safe pair of hands'. This is about delivering the three Cs: conviction, credentials and credibility.
4. Next steps. Show the client that you've thought about the first critical weeks of the engagement and that you're ready to go.

HOW SHOULD YOU WRITE A PROPOSAL EXECUTIVE SUMMARY?

Make it short, simple, punchy and readable. Whatever the topic, an executive summary should score at least 45% readability on the Flesch Reading Ease (FRE) score. Imagine a busy CEO in an elevator with a couple of minutes between floors to 'get' your proposal. Make it easy for them. Pitch your messages at a level they can relate to, i.e. strategic outcomes like ROI, value for money, performance value, organizational goals.

Write more about the client than you. If you must talk about a feature of your product or service, always relate it back to how the client benefits. 'What that means for you is...' will get their attention. **When we talk about ourselves, buyers switch off in (nano)seconds.**

Of course, it's not just a question of creating a shopping list of benefits. Match them to each of the five buyer roles we discussed in Principle 2, or categorize them meaningfully under headings like 'organizational/ strategic', 'financial/commercial', 'functional/operational', 'technical'. You need to make it easy for each evaluator to find the benefits that will most resonate with them.

When writing the benefits, make them specific, concrete and definite. Wherever possible, quantify them. 'A 12% growth in profits over 18 months' is more compelling than 'A significant growth in profits' because it's more precise. Specific benefits give the decision-makers the hard evidence they seek to justify their decision to select you.

Also, consider varying the format and page grid of the executive summary from the body of the document. If you use a single column for the body text, use double columns in the exec summary, or a different typeface. Your goal should be to create an executive summary that can stand on its own, so the CEO or CFO could tear it out of the proposal and read it on the train home... and it would still make sense.

Use graphics. A bar chart, image, graph or photo that supports a key point can be persuasive. Most bids are starved of graphics. Combining numbered lists, bullets and Words in Tables (WiT) works well in an executive summary, as I hope you can see in the re-worked example below.

Here are 'before and after' examples of a proposal executive summary that I worked on with a client (XYZ plc is the name of the buying organization; ABC Ltd, an energy consultancy, is the bidder and my client):

ORIGINAL EXECUTIVE SUMMARY

XYZ plc met with ABC Ltd in 2007 to discuss energy purchasing and invoice validation (Bureau Service) services across its Ireland and UK sites, with Europe to follow.

ABC Ltd has expertise in handling the dynamics of the UK and Irish energy markets. Likewise, our Europe team provides consultancy services in the main European countries such as Netherlands, Belgium, France, Germany, Italy and Spain.

This document describes how ABC Ltd intends to achieve measurable improvements in the management of your energy purchasing and ongoing usage.

To date, ABC Ltd has independently negotiated electricity, gas and water supply for its 30 sites across Ireland and the UK. ABC understands that XYZ's total utility spend is estimated at £10 million per annum.

An internal review of this arrangement has concluded this is not an efficient use of resources.

One solution for XYZ plc is to outsource its energy purchasing requirements to a specialist consultancy. The benefit of this would be the creation of one single supply process. This process can be rolled out across your Europe countries in due course.

Further to agreement, ABC would recommend a flexible energy purchasing strategy through wholesale markets for electricity and gas in the UK.

For Ireland, we recommend a fixed, traditional strategy, until the market has evolved sufficiently to allow use of more flexible products.

Together, these strategies would help provide cost certainty, minimize risk to market price volatility and aim to achieve a lower/acceptable price.

Furthermore, with the growing burden of utility administration weighing heavily on XYZ plc, a new solution to manage this process is required.

A full Bureau Service provides you with an end-to-end management tool for the collection, processing and validation of your utility invoices. This would free up valuable time for your staff and identify possible cost-savings.

Latest research suggests you could be paying more than 10% than you should due to inaccurate invoices. Our Bureau Service would highlight these discrepancies and apply a 'pay and recover' system to recoup your losses.

The top-line objective for you is to integrate your procurement and invoice administration services into one managed solution. This will save you time and present numerous cost-saving opportunities.

A full fee structure is included in Section 5.0. Service Level Agreement with KPIs can be found in Appendix F. At-a-glance costs are provided below:
- Energy procurement for UK and Ireland combined for year one = £65,000 + VAT per annum.
- Bureau Service/Invoice Validation – Electricity, Gas and Water purchasing = £300 + VAT per meter (year one) = £250 + VAT per meter (year two).

European activity will be treated as a separate contract to take into account individual country differences.

ABC Ltd is ready to start work immediately. To proceed with this proposal, please contact John D to discuss further or simply sign the acceptance form and return to us.

CRITIQUE OF THIS ORIGINAL VERSION

Readability Statistics	？ X
Counts	
Words	477
Characters	2605
Paragraphs	19
Sentences	26
Averages	
Sentences per Paragraph	1.6
Words per Sentence	17.2
Characters per Word	5.3
Readability	
Passive Sentences	11%
Flesch Reading Ease	33.9
Flesch-Kincaid Grade Level	12.8
	OK

On the plus side, as you can see from the readability stats above, at 477 words it's short and the ASL (Average Sentence Length) of 17.2 words falls inside the accepted range. But that's about it.

On the minus side, 11% of the sentences are in the passive voice and it only gets an FRE (Flesch Reading Ease) score of 33.9%. This is not good enough for an executive summary, which should be eminently readable and score at least 45% FRE.

Bigger problems by far are the total lack of structure and buried benefits.

Without any sub-headings or signposts, the summary is a string of short, loosely connected paragraphs with no contrast, differentiation or visual interest. This makes it hard for the reader to discern the logic of the argument and find the information they want.

In terms of benefits, I've identified six, plus three features, but the benefits are lost in the text, forcing you to read the entire summary to uncover them. They need to be clear and explicit and jump off the page for the reader.

Here's the final version that the client and I developed together:

REWORKED EXECUTIVE SUMMARY

XYZ plc ('You'/'Your') independently buys electricity, gas and water ('utilities') for its 50 sites across Ireland and the UK. You have estimated that your total utility spend is £10 million a year. An internal review has concluded that you could be managing this process better and saving up to £750,000 per year.

OUR UNDERSTANDING OF YOUR NEEDS
Based on your RFP and discussions with Steve M and Debbie Y, we understand that you seek:
1. An end-to-end process that improves your approach to buying utilities and managing invoice administration.
2. Cost certainty and effective risk management in your energy purchasing strategy.
3. To identify overcharging errors and cost-saving opportunities through state-of-the-art invoice validation software and techniques.

HOW WE PROPOSE TO MEET YOUR NEEDS
We recommend you outsource your entire energy purchasing and invoice administration to ABC Ltd. We would deliver this to you in four ways:

1. Using our Bureau Service will improve how you manage your invoices, saving your business money and your people time. We specifically recommend you use our Bureau Services to:
   - ✓ Create and maintain your own site database
   - ✓ Collect, process and validate your utility invoices
   - ✓ Stamp and 'journal' your utility invoices for payment
   - ✓ Handle any pay and recover opportunities to save you money.

   You will get protection from overcharging. We use our proprietary software ('ICMAS') to process and validate your invoices, allowing us to pick up any amended small print that could compromise you. We process up to 30,000 invoices a month and keep up-to-date with suppliers' invoicing procedures, alerting you to material changes in their terms and conditions.

   Our research (see Appendix D) of 11 corporate customers suggests you could be paying 10% more than you should, due to inaccurate invoices. In 2011, we validated our customers' invoices and saved them a total of £2.5m.

2. You will get expert advice from Tim Y, your own dedicated energy trader, on the most appropriate energy purchasing strategy. Your need for cost certainty and risk management will drive the agenda of every meeting with Tim.

3. In the UK, you will be able to buy and sell from the market at opportune moments through the flexible energy purchasing strategy that we recommend for you, using our 'Lock/Unlock' product. Based on your consumption figures for 2011, we calculate that, had you used this product with us, you could have saved up to 0.53p per K/Wh.

4. In Ireland, you will get cost certainty through the fixed, traditional energy purchasing strategy that we recommend for you. Once the Irish energy market has settled down, we can use more bespoke products, such as the 'Day/Month Ahead', for you. Appendix A explains in more detail how this works.

OUR PROPOSED FEES

A full fee structure is in Section 5.0. To deliver the benefits you have told us you seek – cost certainty, effective risk management, major cost-savings, generous deals negotiated for you, protection from overcharging, early warning of pitfalls and risky offers, an efficient energy purchasing strategy and the reassurance that you are in safe, expert hands – we propose charging you the following fees:

1. Energy procurement for UK and Ireland for year 1:
   £65,000 + VAT per annum
2. Bureau Service for electricity, gas and water purchasing:
   £300 + VAT per meter in year 1
   £250 + VAT per meter in year 2.

WHY ABC LTD?

WHAT YOU GET	HOW AND WHY YOU GET IT
Comfort, reassurance, peace of mind	Our Energy Trading team is one of only two in the UK to hold Financial Services Authority (FSA) accreditation. You get the comfort of dealing with an inspected, accredited organization keen to maintain its high standards and strong reputation in the market.
The best deals in the market	Our 15-strong Energy Trading team – some of whom you have met – has over 100 years' combined experience in buying gas and electricity. This team has the knowledge and experience to spot and deliver market opportunities early for you. They can also give you early warning of pitfalls and risky offers. Managing over £800m worth of energy gives us clout in the marketplace, allowing us to negotiate generous deals for you.
Better prices	We created the Wholesale Power Purchasing approach (see Appendix A) in 2003 to help clients like you get better prices on the 'open' market.
Large annual savings	Our ICMAS software can process over 100,000 invoices a month. By staying on top of suppliers' billing procedures and the tiniest changes to their small print, we can validate a large number of invoices and protect you from overcharging. On average we save our customers £5,000 a year.

PROPOSED NEXT STEPS

We will address your European activity in a separate proposal at your request. We're ready to start work immediately. Assuming this is acceptable to you, John D will contact you within the next five working days to discuss this proposal further, answer any questions you may have and schedule your first meeting with Tim Y.

CRITIQUE OF THIS FINAL VERSION

Readability Statistics	?	X
Counts		
Words		763
Characters		3816
Paragraphs		27
Sentences		38
Averages		
Sentences per Paragraph		2.2
Words per Sentence		17.7
Characters per Word		4.8
Readability		
Passive Sentences		0%
Flesch Reading Ease		47.6
Flesch-Kincaid Grade Level		10.9
		OK

As you can see, it's totally different from the original version and much more powerful because:

- The opening paragraph grabs the reader's attention by describing their chief needs and a major cost-saving opportunity
- The client benefits are numbered, explicit and in some cases quantified
- The structure is clear and simple
- 'You' and 'your' feature more prominently
- There are no sentences in the passive voice
- The language is simpler, e.g. 'buy' instead of 'purchase'

WHEN SHOULD WE WRITE THE EXECUTIVE SUMMARY?

Some people like to write it last, so they know what's in the proposal to summarize. But if you run out of time and rush it, it'll read like an afterthought. You might prefer to write it first, to force yourself to think through why the client should select you, then use the rest of the proposal to support it. In practice, however, it's hard to complete the executive summary before you've written the rest of the proposal, as the act of writing the content helps you develop and refine your ideas and arguments.

My recommendation (and my experience) is to build your exec summary as you go. As you assemble the body of the proposal, note the strongest arguments for selecting you, usually the client benefits. When the time comes to write the summary, they'll be clearer in your head and faster to draft.

HOW LONG SHOULD IT BE?

Personal view here, but no longer than three pages. Any more than that and it becomes just another section in the document. Remember: you're summarizing, not expanding on or building an argument.

WINNER TAKES ALL
BOTTOM LINE:

Even in good times, winning bids and tenders is ferociously competitive, with decisions often made on marginal differences between bidders. In the current climate, winning is even tougher, especially if the client's decision is based solely on your written response. Fronting your bid with a clear, concise, compelling and benefits-laden executive summary is a great way of widening the gap between you and the competition.

FOOD FOR THOUGHT

Score your latest executive summary out of 10, where 1 = strongly disagree with the following statements and 10 = strongly agree:

The structure of my exec summary is logical, clear, explicit	/10
The client benefits are clear, explicit and quantified	/10
There is abundant use of 'you', 'your' and the client's name	/10
The summary is readable (10 points for an FRE of 60%+, 5 points for 45%+ and 1 point for < 45%)	/10
TOTAL:	/40

If you scored 40, well done. If you scored 30-39, good, but you could do better. If you scored less than 30, please re-read this chapter or consider attending one of my workshops on executive summaries (**http://bit.ly/2jTzskg**).

principle

5

Present a
powerful pitch

1. The purpose of the pitch.
2. Which pitch slot to take.
3. Designing and practising your pitch.
4. Debriefing your pitch.
5. Some myths about presenting.

PURPOSE: WHAT'S THE PITCH (OR PRESENTATION) FOR?

A pitch is a formal, face-to-face presentation to the client of your proposed solution or value proposition. Its purpose is not to entertain, educate, inform, introduce new team members or recap the document. It's to persuade the client to appoint you. And it's your last chance to do so.

You do that by answering all their doubts, concerns and questions, and by convincing them that you are as good as you said you were in the bid document (if there was one). To win, you need to ensure that the client answers 'yes' to these questions about you:

- 'Do they offer us more value for money than any other bidder?'
- 'Do they understand us and our business?'
- 'Are they a team?'
- 'Are they keen to work with us?'
- 'Can we work with them?'

Also known as the 'beauty parade' or 'interview', the pitch is probably the only time that all of them will meet all of you. So they're likely to make things tough for you, because they want to see how you fare under pressure, how well you think on your feet and how strong a team you are. They'll stress-test you, seeking reasons to reject you. Many teams have blown it at this stage with a lacklustre presentation, while other teams have come from behind to snatch the win.

It's all about your performance on the day. It's a stage-managed theatrical show, with a cast, lines, steps and choreography... and you've got to get it all right. The client will extrapolate your performance and their impression of you on the day to what it will be like working with you in the weeks and months ahead. **Pitching is a brief, intense and pivotal experience. It's the shooting star of business development.**

WHICH PITCH SLOT TO TAKE

So you need to prepare thoroughly. But you can't do that until and unless you know how long you've got to present, which slot you've been given, what you're going to say and who's going to say it.

If you have any choice at all over your slot, ask the client if you can go either first or last.

If all the pitches are due to take place over a short period, like a day, then go first. Based on the theory of primacy, the thinking behind this is that you will set the tone and the standard for the other bidders to follow. If you're brilliant, the client may decide there and then to appoint you.

If, however, the presentations are held over a longer period, like a week, then it's best to go last, based on the theory of recency. The client is more likely to remember the last presentation they heard on Friday than the first one on Monday. But going last at the end of a gruelling week for the client has implications for content and length. You may want to cut to the chase (solution + client benefits) even sooner than you originally intended, to keep their attention and make their decision easy.

DESIGNING AND PRACTISING YOUR PITCH

How much time is your presentation slot? An hour? However much or little time the client has given you, you've got less than you think.

Research conducted by the Learning Point Presentations School found that **the proportion of the client's final decision attributed to the formal presentation is a mere 25%**; the Q&A accounts for a whacking 75%! That's because the client thinks that in the Q&A they're seeing you 'unplugged', in the raw. What they don't know is that you've worked your socks off anticipating 90% of their likely questions and prepping your answers.

So if your slot is 60 minutes, you need to prepare a 15- to 20-minute presentation, with the remaining time allotted to the Q&A. This has profound implications for what you prioritize and how you allocate your prep time.

Let's deal with the formal presentation first.

'WHO'S MY PITCH TEAM?'

Your first major decision is whom to take. The team you take to the presentation should be dictated by whom the client is expecting to see, i.e. the team roles that matter most to them.

Find out (by asking) who will attend from the client and match them with your people in terms of role, grade, experience, style and culture. This is the same concept of mirroring/level-selling that we explored in Principle 3: 'Meet the client pre-submission'. Each member of the client panel needs to recognize their opposite number on your team.

If you've had pre-submission meetings with the client and they've gone well, it makes sense for the same people to present. The client will recognize them and be comfortable with them.

If for any reason you decide to involve a new team member in the pitch, give the client early warning of that and, if you can, introduce the new person to them beforehand. If that's not possible, at the very least explain to the client why you are adding them to the team and what they bring to the party. New people fielded at this stage will find it much harder to build rapport than in those earlier meetings, due to the formality of the pitch event.

There must be logic and balance in your team selection too, with both apparent to the client. And everyone you take must speak. Don't be tempted to take 'bag-carriers' or note-takers. I was once involved in a pitch where the senior partner decided to take his secretary to record the meeting. In the debrief after we'd learnt that we'd lost, the client wondered why she was there and added that he'd found her silent presence a distraction.

Also – and forgive me if this is obvious – it doesn't make sense to take someone just to answer a certain type of question in the Q&A if they don't also have a part in the formal presentation. If that question doesn't come up, they'll have sat there looking (and probably feeling) redundant.

Your team needs to be culturally appropriate, too. I once heard about a consultancy bidding for a local authority contract to advise them on workforce diversity. The bid team comprised four white, middle-aged men… who had to present to a panel of ethnically diverse women in their 20s and 30s. Oops.

Though not a tendering example, a printing company I know run solely by Muslims was sent a Christmas hamper full of wine and chutneys by one of their clients. A box of chocolates at Eid would have been more thoughtful.

WHAT TYPES OF DECISION-MAKER CAN YOU EXPECT TO SEE ON THE CLIENT PANEL?

Broad brush, the client panel will usually comprise representatives of the five typical buyer roles that we explored in Principle 3. Here's a quick reminder:

THE BOSS	The ultimate authority and decision-maker. Motivated to achieve strategic, organizational goals; often visionary. Their assessment of you will tend to be: **strategic.**
THE MONEY PERSON	Signs the cheques. Able to allocate funds and release or withhold budgets. Interested in ROI. Their assessment of you will tend to be: **commercial.**
THE END-USER	Uses or manages the product or service regularly. Interested in features, functionality, ease of use, reliability. Their assessment of you will tend to be: **operational.**
THE EXPERT	Has deep technical understanding of the product or service and its competitors. Interested in features, supply, application, future-proofing. Their assessment of you will tend to be: **technical.**
THE GUIDE/ THE ENFORCER	May or may not be a user of the product or service. If external, they may be a consultant brought in by The Boss to give informed, objective advice. If internal, they are likely to be from Procurement. If external, their assessment of you will tend to be: **pragmatic, i.e. whatever helps justify their involvement in the process.** If Procurement, their assessment of you will tend to be: **price-based.**

If you asked for and got meetings with the client pre-submission, you should already have sussed out who occupies each of these roles. If not, you'll be hard pushed in the pitch to match your people accurately with theirs.

If you submitted a written document, you will already have developed win-themes and main messages, so designing the message content of your pitch should be relatively easy. But you also need to overlay those messages onto the five hot buying buttons identified in the table above: strategic, commercial, operational, technical, and pragmatic/cost. This will not only influence what you say, but how you say it. So take the members of your team most appropriate to give those messages and press those buttons. This is not about charisma, but the most logical presenters to give those messages.

At the very least, the people who must attend the pitch are:

- The captain of your team, i.e. whoever leads your bid and is answerable for delivery and overall service quality
- Whomever the client will see most of in the delivery of the contract, e.g. the audit team, the training deliverers, the merger team, the legal associates
- A product/service expert who can answer the client's technical concerns.

Bringing in the great and the good at the last minute is risky

Avoid wheeling in a senior person at this stage of the tender process, unless there is a very good reason to do so. This can disrupt the team's internal bonds and the client's perception of you as a team. A senior person brought in to rescue a flagging bid can also dominate proceedings, again destroying the teamwork carefully nurtured over weeks or months.

In their bid to host the 2012 Olympics, France brought in the Paris mayor, Jacques Chirac, at the 11th hour to show commitment to their pledges in the bid document. Leaks from inside the French camp claimed, however, that this move undermined the *esprit de corps* that the team had developed over many months of working together. And we all know who won the bid to host the 2012 Olympics.

Another example was England's 2011 bid to host the 2018 FIFA Football World Cup. Despite the charm offensive of David Cameron, David Beckham and Prince William, it was all too late to change the minds of the FIFA Executive Committee members. Most of them had already decided whom they were going to vote for. Trying to change their minds in the last few days was always going to be an uphill struggle, with the added risk that they would perceive it as a sign of desperation.

STRUCTURING YOUR PITCH

Having decided who's going to present, you need to structure the formal, stand-up presentation. Here's my anatomy of a competitive pitch:

1. A powerful opening.
2. Brief introduction of your team and their proposed roles on the assignment.
3. Brief re-statement of the client's needs, goals, issues or challenges.
4. Your proposed solution and its benefits to the client.
5. (optional) Brief credentials, e.g. where you've done this before and the results you achieved for the client.
6. Summary and close.

Let's dissect each section.

1. The opening.
Usually the job of the team leader, how you open your pitch is vital. Some say this is the most important part, as it sets the scene and the tone, and grabs the audience's attention. If you lose the client early on, you may never get them back. Consider a story, quote, statistic or physical prop.

A THUMPING GOOD OPENING

One of the most striking pitch openers I've ever seen was by an engineering company. Led by their MD, the team entered the room carrying a large iron anvil, with a gold plaque on its plinth. They lowered it carefully and silently onto a felt mat laid across the mahogany boardroom table. The client was spellbound.

The MD of the bidding company, an imposing man, laid his hands on top of the anvil, made deliberate eye contact with each member of the client panel and said, 'Ladies and gentlemen, we won this last year for being the most innovative small engineering company in the UK. Please allow me to introduce my team.' Their presentation was slick, the Q&A well prepared, and they won the contract.

---

2. Team introduction.
Either you can introduce your team, or even better, let each person introduce themselves. That gives them airtime and gets them involved in the pitch quickly. Your mission should be to get to sections 3 and 4 as quickly as possible, so this section needs to be snappy. Learn it off by heart.

3. Re-statement of the client's needs, goals, issues or challenges.
Again, this needs to be non-controversial, brief and succinct. The reason this section of your pitch is important is that it sets the scene for your solution, especially for anyone on the panel who either hasn't read your bid document or has entered the process late. Assume the client has not read your document cover to cover.

4. Your proposed solution.
This is the guts of your pitch, your value proposition, and where you need to spend most of your time. This should include your approach (expressed in a 'killer slide'), roles and responsibilities, outcomes, outputs, benefits to

the client, and price. Here you answer the client's question, 'WIIFM?' Link the benefits closely to the price, i.e. 'This is what you pay and this is what you get for that investment'.

5. Your credentials.
The reason I think this is optional is because it takes time away from section 4, your proposed solution. If you do a good enough job presenting it, that in itself will 'credentialize' you. It's unlikely the client will have invited you to pitch if they didn't think you could do the job. So if you're pushed for time and you're looking for stuff to cut, cut this.

6. The ending.
The task of closing and summarizing the pitch often falls to the team leader, i.e. they top and tail the formal presentation. If in doubt, recap all the juicy benefits the client will get if they appoint you. Answer their 'WIIFM?' question and remind them how badly you want to be the organization that delivers those benefits. Don't be afraid to ask for the business.

THE 'KILLER' IDEA
Every new business pitch should have what I call a 'killer idea' or 'Big Idea' – usually a graphic – that encapsulates your value proposition, especially for a complex service. This anchors and unifies your pitch, allowing your speakers to refer to it and illustrate their individual role in its delivery. I spoke at length about this in Principle 3: 'Meet the Client Pre-Submission': this is the initial service model or outline concept that you test with the client in your pre-submission meetings.

Here's one used by a healthcare provider in a pitch to Her Majesty's Prison Service for prisoner medical services in a region of the UK:

Don't worry too much about the detail, but suffice to say that the centre of the graphic shows their core services, with 24/7 medical cover for prisoners at the apex. The boxes surrounding the pyramid represent various elements of the service and key stakeholders, while the white boxes on the outer edge are the broader supporting organizations, such as mental health and social services.

The bid team and I spent half a day together building this graphic. In their pitch, the graphic formed the core of their presentation and the major talking point in the Q&A. It unified, clarified and summarized their proposition to the client.

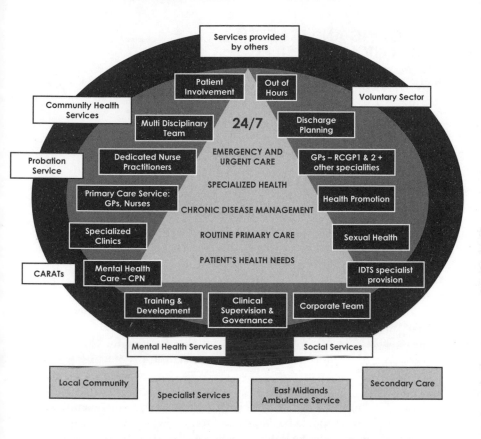

A PICTURE IS WORTH A THOUSAND WORDS

To quote another example from the bid to host the 2018 FIFA Football World Cup, the client, FIFA, stated that they wanted to open up new frontiers in world football. The self-proclaimed 'home of football' – England – is clearly not a new frontier.

One of the slides in Russia's presentation, the eventual winner of the bid, was a map of Europe, with a line separating Russia from western Europe. To the left of the line were all the venues of previous World Cups; to the right, nothing.

One simple graphic conveyed Russia's entire message, which chimed with the client's own objective.

DESIGNING AND PRACTISING
YOUR PITCH: FOUR STEPS

Having structured your pitch (i.e. you know who is presenting and in what order), you now need to design it and practise delivering it. This happens in four steps:

1. The design walk-through
2. First rehearsal
3. Dress rehearsal
4. Final dress rehearsal.

Scheduling and coordinating these meetings usually falls to the bid manager. They book the rehearsal room and schedule rehearsal time in everyone's diaries, making sure everyone turns up and every presenter goes through their piece. Though this is rare, some bid managers also act as a presentation coach.

1. Design walk-through

Having agreed who will present and in what order, get together with your fellow presenters and walk through the likely content in the form of scribbled presentations, notes or draft slides. Agree the main messages, overall running order and approximate timing. Start designing the pitch.

If you've submitted a bid document as part of the process, identifying your key messages should be easy. If not, you'll need to spend much more time agreeing and refining those as section 4 of your pitch, your proposed solution. Developing those themes or messages may call for more research, which in turn could affect the design.

Besides the presenters, other stakeholders could be involved in this meeting, to pitch in their views on content and style.

The theatre or cinema analogy to this meeting is the read-through. The actors and director read from the script and discuss the main themes of each speech or scene. This may include the choreography, i.e. where the actors begin and end physically and emotionally, sometimes referred to as the 'arc' of a scene.

Each presenter should leave the design walk-through with homework: to develop his/her slides ready for the First Rehearsal.

2. First Rehearsal

If everyone has done their homework, you will all re-convene with more developed slides. You know more or less what you want to say, but it's still rough around the edges. You half-present, half-walk through your slides, depending on your level of confidence, and you use the input of your colleagues to help you refine them further. But your focus is still on your own individual bit, rather than the pitch as a whole.

If at this stage you're struggling to clarify what you mean or to define a clear message, my advice is always the same: write it down or say it as if you were talking to your best friend. Expressing a thought or idea in writing forces you to clarify it: you're literally putting it in black and white. Or buddy up with a team member and explain to them in conversational language what you mean. Verbalizing in simple language will help you distil your ideas.

3. Dress rehearsal

This rehearsal is where it all starts to come together. By now, you and your fellow presenters should be totally familiar with your piece. With the stopwatch on, you run through the whole pitch several times with your slides, visual aids and props, and assess it as a team. Typically at this stage you'll be fine-tuning your presentations and the words/ graphics on the slides, shaving off a few seconds here, adding a few more there.

In this rehearsal, teams tend to make a gear change and focus on making the handovers seamless and the timing precise. Make sure that the top and tail of your pitch are clear, concise and compelling.

By now, you should be able to capture the structure, messages and timings of your pitch like this:

SPEAKER	MESSAGES	TIME
TIM	**We understand you and your issues** Introduce team and roles (briefly). Say how each will speak a little about each area. Overview of the business: - achieved a lot - where they see themselves - mention of factory visit and drop some names of our staff and their staff - key audit requirements and tax considerations - considering them as a listed company - how our role fits their evolving needs	4 mins

FIONA	Continuity, familiarity and she's got it planned and controlled Priority tasks to concentrate on: - Getting things going immediately, incorporating the planning for listed status - Refer to areas and people like they are neighbours and colleagues - Refer specifically to controls/systems we know and how we can immediately contribute - We are in an excellent position to audit the opening balance sheet and prepare for the flotation as we proceed with the audit	4 mins
JOHN	We know (your) factories - Observations on the factories - Parallels with another situation and the benefits that can be produced (very brief)	4 mins
RICHARD	We know flotations from the MBO point of view and understand your perspective - Key issues facing them with specifics about the company (briefly) - War story emphasizing the role of early planning, keys to success and how they achieved high value - Offer reference	5 mins
TIM	We are the team that knows you and can guide you into the future Summary points: - an audit where you know us and can rely on our knowledge and well-managed coordination - Tim is a hands-on, in-touch partner with commercial insight into evolving issues of a developing business - can identify time and relevance for specialist input - accounting issues related to listed status addressed early and systematically - working with you on operational efficiency, preparing for a successful flotation We look forward to discussing your views and clarifying any points	3 mins
TOTAL:		20 mins

If steps 1 and 2 are about creating the jigsaw pieces, step 3 is about putting them all together.

4. Final dress rehearsal
This is where the magic happens.

Every presenter should know their material so well that they have internalized it; it's become part of them. Here physical actions and words become inextricably linked, individual presenters transcend their own content, see beyond their own particular role… and become a team. This is when the pitch gains an impact beyond the sum of its parts.

In my experience, this is also where a decisive shift in mindset can take place: the team moves from being bidder-centric to being buyer-centric. They start using the magic words 'you' and 'your' more than 'I', 'we' or 'us'. Their emotional and intellectual focus moves from themselves to the client. And that can take a pitch from good to great.

When designing your pitch, limit the number of ideas

Another word of advice when you're designing your pitch: less is more. Just because you're desperate to win doesn't mean you have to throw everything at it, including the kitchen sink. Confine each presenter to three or four main ideas; there's a limit to the amount of information that people can absorb when it's delivered orally. If you bombard the client with too many ideas, you run the risk of losing them and your main message, particularly if yours is the umpteenth pitch they've heard that day.

And remember the power of story: anecdotes, war stories, examples and case studies all bring your proposition alive for the client. Stories humanize dry facts and figures, convey emotion and, if well told, stay long in the memory.

Why is practising so important?
If you want to win, it's not optional.

By 'practise' I mean standing up and delivering your piece, both by yourself in front of the mirror and with your team-mates. Simply reading your notes or slides, either to yourself or in a 'walk-through' with your colleagues, will not cut it. Practising the night before won't cut it. Nor will going through it in the cab on the way there!

There's no substitute for proper rehearsals well before you're on.

If you're in any doubt as to why you should practise, try these benefits for size. Rehearsing allows you to:
• Refine your content, both orally and on your slides
• Establish the precise running order
• Refine your answers in the Q&A
• Clarify handovers and timing

- Gain confidence
- Relax and be natural
- Forget yourself and focus on the client
- Spot gaps or problems and fix them.

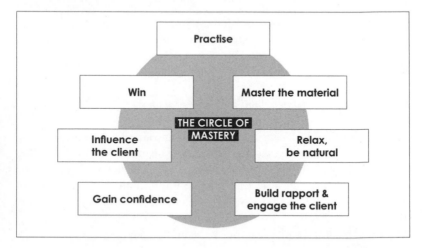

The entry point into this virtuous circle is practice.

A gentle warning, however.

Don't over-practise. In the same way that you can over-stretch a muscle, you can over-rehearse a pitch. You must practise enough to master the material and the choreography of the show, but not so much that you get fed up with it, stale or tired.

Not only must you practise your own individual section of the formal presentation, you must also anticipate the questions likely to come up in the Q&A and your answers (more of that later).

Overcoming nerves with practice

One of the biggest challenges in a pitch is nerves. In my experience, most presenters get nervous because they lack confidence in their content. Practising and mastering your content – spotting things that are unclear or irrelevant and correcting them – turns uncertainty into certainty and boosts confidence.

As a trainer, I present to groups of people all the time and am highly confident. But when I look back to presentations early in my career where

I've been extremely nervous, without exception it's been because I've lacked confidence in my content. So if you know your stuff and are presenting on that topic, there's no reason not to be confident.

You will find that the very act of rehearsing your piece forces you to clarify and refine it, in your own head, orally and on the slides. The clearer it is in your head, the clearer it will be when you verbalize it.

But I don't want you to learn a script that you trot out verbatim: that will render your presentation lifeless and robotic. I want you to be so familiar with your content, the ideas and the order in which you'll present them that, however your brain spontaneously chooses to express them, they come out clearly and concisely. So, on the day of the pitch, the only prompt you'll need is a couple of 4 x 6-inch index cards with your notes of the main messages.

Using an external presentation coach

Steps 3 and 4 are also where the right coach or consultant can take your pitch to the next level. They can help you to vary the pace and cadence; turn a good story into a great one; clarify or enliven content that is vague or dull; challenge inappropriate, clichéd or sloppy language; champion plain English (the panel may include lay staff who won't get the technical jargon); dispense individual coaching to people who know their stuff but are not natural presenters; praise people who are doing well; and tell the senior partner to stop dominating if they want to win!

An external coach who can establish credibility quickly and build rapport with the team brings an objectivity to rehearsals and supports the team with comments, ideas, suggestions and feedback. They can do and say things that most bid managers might not feel able to, due to inexperience, lack of confidence or their relationship with the bid team.

A good external coach can also lay down the law when they need to, e.g. insisting that everyone on the team practise, especially those who don't think they need to (you know who you are).

I've coached senior partners in professional services who thought they could wing it because they'd done so many pitches before and knew what to do. But what message would their absence send to the more junior members of the team? That it's OK to abandon best practice when you reach a certain level in the firm? And how about building teamwork, mucking in with your more junior colleagues and showing them how it's done?

The real truth is often that they're scared of presenting in front of their peers and showing themselves up. What they don't appreciate is that a leader who's prepared to reveal some vulnerability to their team gets respect, not scorn.

Slide design

As you're likely to use PowerPoint in your pitch, it's worth saying a few words about it.

Several years ago, an MIT study found that 73% of business communication was conducted via PowerPoint. Despite this huge usage, PowerPoint slides tend to be badly designed and presented.

The most common design mistake is what Garr Reynolds describes in his book Presentation Zen (2008) as 'slideuments': slides crammed with dense bullet points copied and pasted from a document. The presenter then proceeds to use the slide show as a teleprompt, reading out every word on the slide with their back to the audience.

Not only is this rude, it's also ineffective. Research from the University of New South Wales (Sweller, 2007) indicates that it's harder to process information if it's presented orally and visually at the same time. Reading a list of bullet points out loud from the screen actually inhibits your audience's ability to digest that information. If you want your audience to read a slide, stop speaking. Take a breath, count to five, then resume.

Slides are a visual aid; they are not your pitch. It's a cliché, but the most important visual aid in a presentation is the presenter. You should be more interesting than your slides. And you should know your presentation well enough to be able to present without them.

Here are some basic tips on slide design:
- Less is more
- Have no more than six bullet points on a slide
- Keep the text of each bullet to six words or fewer
- Use more graphics (images, charts, tables, graphs) than words
- Make the graphics simple and clear
- Use colour to clarify, not decorate.

STORY:
BAD SLIDES CAN KILL

On 1 February 2003, the seven astronauts on board the space shuttle Columbia died when their aircraft disintegrated on re-entry into Earth's atmosphere.

The cause of the catastrophe was damage sustained during launch when a piece of foam insulation the size of a small briefcase broke off from one of the external tanks. The debris struck the leading edge of the left wing, damaging the tiles of the Shuttle's Thermal Protection System (TPS), which shields it from the intense heat generated during re-entry.

Could this disaster have been prevented?

According to the findings of an information design expert, a poorly written and overladen PowerPoint slide failed to alert NASA engineers to the danger.

A week before the disaster, a Debris Assessment Team delivered a formal briefing on PowerPoint. While the team warned of the huge risk of debris damage at take-off, the message never got through.

According to information design expert Edward Tufte, Professor Emeritus at Yale, the structure, layout and language of the key slide made it nearly impossible to decode the message. Out of 17 fact-filled lines on the slide, the main message was buried at the end:

"Flight condition is significantly outside of test database Volume of ramp is 1920cu in vs 3 cu in for test."

In plain English, this means that the debris that struck the wing was 640 times greater than the data used to calibrate the model to predict the tile damage. The model was flawed. And the word 'significant' here (an over-used word if ever there was one) means:

"So much damage that everyone dies."

If the slide had been that direct, the seven astronauts might still be alive today.

Taken directly from the *Columbia* Accident Investigation Board report, here's the slide that failed to communicate the risk of debris damage at take-off (the arrows point to particularly confusing elements of the slide in Professor Tufte's analysis):

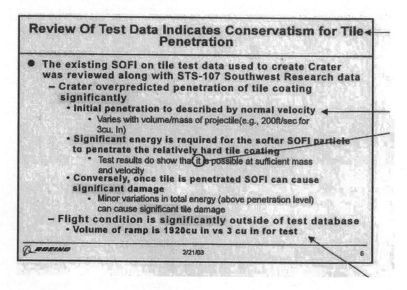

x The title of the slide is misleading: it doesn't refer to the predicted tile damage, but to the choice of test models used to predict the damage.

x Six levels of hierarchy created by the bullet points and dashes make it hard to prioritize the information

x The vaguely quantitative words 'significant' and 'significantly' appear five times, each with different meanings

x The same volume metric (cubic inches) is shown three different ways: 3cu.In, 1920cu in, 3 cu in – in highly technical fields like aerospace engineering, a misplaced decimal point or unit of measurement can have serious repercussions

x The vague pronoun reference 'it' alludes to damage to the protective tiles, which caused the destruction of the *Columbia*.

The high-level NASA engineers tasked with assessing the risk of wing damage were satisfied that the reports – including this slide – indicated that *Columbia* was not in danger. Tragically, no further action was taken.

IF YOU HAVE TO USE POWERPOINT, USE IT WELL
Here are a few tips for getting the most out of PowerPoint.

When in 'slideshow' mode:
- For a list of tips: press Fn + F1
- To blacken the screen: press the 'B' key; press it again to restore the slide
- To whiten the screen: press the 'W' key; press it again to restore the slide
- To hide the arrow: press the 'A' key; press it again to bring it back
- To go to the start or end of your presentation: press the 'Home' or 'End' keys
- Number your slides and keep a list handy: if you press a number and 'Enter', you'll immediately go to that slide
- Put a blank slide at the end of your presentation: this will stop the slideshow from reverting to whatever embarrassing picture is on your desktop when you shut it down
- To toggle between showing the slide only on the computer screen, showing it on both the computer and the big screen, and showing it only on the big screen: press 'Fn' + F1 or F5 or F7 (depending on your computer brand)
- To select an object, picture or text, or add a hyperlink to another slide, presentation or website: press 'Ctrl' + K
- To end the slideshow: press 'Esc'.

AN ALTERNATIVE TO SLIDES?

Just because millions of people around the world resort to slides (usually PowerPoint) doesn't mean you have to. I've known buyers to heave a sigh of relief when a bidder has asked them if it would be OK not to use Power-Point in their presentation (we've all suffered 'death by PowerPoint' at least once in our careers, and once is enough).

A viable alternative to slides is flipcharts.

Akin to storyboards much used in advertising and media, I've seen flip-charts used in a pitch, with a combination of pre-prepared and 'impro-vised/spontaneous' flips seemingly produced on the fly – though, in reality, well practised – to illustrate key points.

This bold alternative to slides only works, however, if you practise produc-ing and presenting them, as you would with any presentation. Otherwise they can appear 'home-made' and amateurish.

Slides, storyboards, flipcharts – they are all only visual aids to support your messages. They are not the messages themselves. If your content is irrele-vant, generic or dull, your mode of communication is immaterial. Fancy delivery won't hide rubbish content.

PREPPING THE Q&A

We established a few pages back that this part of the pitch can account for up to 75% of the client's final decision.

Prepping this session means anticipating the likeliest and toughest questions, building the best possible answers, deciding which member(s) of your team should answer them and practising giving those answers.

Everybody on the team must be clear about what type of questions they can or should answer in the Q&A session, as well as who may give a secondary or back-up answer in those question areas, where necessary.

This gives team members equal airtime and reduces the chances of one person dominating. It also demonstrates to the client that team members are knowledgeable on subjects outside their primary area. Finally, it underlines teamwork by ensuring that some questions are answered by more than one person.

As with the formal presentation, this is not about learning answers by rote. It's about driving clarity into who answers which types of question and how best to answer them.

ANTICIPATE 90% OF THE CLIENT'S QUESTIONS

We know that the most common questions fit the five roles of the buying group described earlier, i.e. strategic, commercial, operational, technical, and pragmatic/price-based.

Strategic questions may be about your vision for the client's organization, the extent of your ambition for them, their strengths and weaknesses, how you see the market developing and why, the competition and the biggest threats to the client. A good way of prepping strategic questions is to do a SWOT (strengths, weaknesses, opportunities and threats) analysis on the client: this will cover most of the likely angles of attack and impress The Boss that you've done your homework.

Commercial questions will focus on price and its relationship with the benefits offered, possible discounts, the likely return on investment, value over the whole contract lifetime, likely payback period and profitability.

Operational questions centre on how your product or service will be delivered and used, how it will fit in with existing programmes or services, and how, where and when client staff will experience it.

Technical questions will tend to look more deeply at how the product works, its specification, dimensions, supply, modifications, models, 'future-proofability'.

Pragmatic questions are often the 10% that we struggle to anticipate, and therefore the hardest to deal with. Often posed by The Guide/The Enforcer, who may be trying to impress The Boss, these questions come out of left field and aim to throw you. They range from 'What distinguishes you from the other bidders?' and 'Why should we appoint you?' to a pointed question to a junior team member on a point of detail. If they find a weakness in your presentation, they'll go for you. Think of them as a bloodhound.

And if The Guide is from Procurement, you can be pretty sure that they will question you on price/cost, discounts and value for money.

LOGISTICS AND PREPARATION
HANDOUTS: WHEN TO HAND THEM OUT?

Most clients will expect some form of documentation at the pitch, at the very least a copy of your slides in the form of a slide booklet. The big debate is when to hand it out: at the start or at the end?

My firm advice on this is at the start, for the main reason that the client can make notes on the relevant slide pages as you deliver the presentation. I've seen clients receiving a so-called 'leave-behind' at the end complain that they weren't given it at the beginning, for that very reason.

I know you may be concerned that handing it out up-front encourages them to flick ahead to the price slide. Let them do that; you can't exactly stop them, can you? But indulge them for a few seconds, then contract with them up-front to take questions at the end and bring them gently back to slide 1 by holding up a copy of the handout open on that page.

Most clients are happy when they hear that you're only going to present for 20 minutes and then answer their questions for the remaining 40. They know they're going to be able to ask all the tough questions – what they don't know is that you've anticipated them and prepped your answers!

SEATING AND OTHER LOGISTICS

I said earlier that a good pitch has a clear choreography: everyone knows what they're meant to be doing and when. And that includes who sits where and why. Here's a salutary tale for how little things unheeded can trip you up:

A SEDENTARY TALE

I once sat on the client side as a Guide/Enforcer reviewing pitches for a training contract. The presentation room was nice enough, but slightly cramped as there were too many tables and chairs in it from a previous meeting.

One of the bidding favourites came in to present. The team of five filed in, full of confidence and brio, and approached the table they were to present from, which had the standard bottles of mineral water and glasses neatly placed across it, with a data projector centre-stage.

Unfortunately, because the gap between the table and the wall behind it was quite small, they had little room to manoeuvre. It wouldn't have been a problem if they'd been clear about who was sitting where. But they weren't.

The MD sat down rather thoughtlessly in the middle seat, forcing his colleagues to negotiate the wafer-thin space between him and the wall, two of whom went for the same seat at exactly the same time. One of them lost his footing, stumbled and, reaching out for support in an increasingly unstable world, crashed into the table, sending bottles, glasses and water flying over pads, notes and slide booklets. Oops.

On the other side of the room we sat back and watched the disaster unfold, half-horrified, half-amused at their self-destruction. In a nano-second our perception of them and their likely appointment had changed.

Clearly thrown, their confidence visibly draining away and the MD looking as if he was having an out-of-body experience, they'd lost before they'd even begun.

The take-home message is clear: agree in advance who's going to sit where. Instinct may tell you that your bid leader always sits in the centre of the team. Why not be bold and let them sit to the side or on the edge? From their role on the day it will still be apparent to the client that he or she is the leader, but it might also send the client a subtle message about humility and self-effacement.

When it comes to more junior members of the team, avoid placing them on the edge or to the side. That may make them look (and feel) forgotten or under-valued. Show that they are integrated in the team by putting them in or near the centre. And colleagues who will work together on the contract should probably sit together.

> *"If they can't manage a harmonious presentation,*
> *would we trust them with our worldwide audit?"*
> A multinational client

But seating is far from the only thing that can go wrong.

What do you do if the data projector blows up, or the bulb goes? You either take a spare, or you're so well prepared you're happy to present without slides (another reason for having a slide booklet).

What happens if the client has positioned you in the room miles from the nearest power point? You bring an extension lead.

What happens if you're presenting overseas? You make sure you take an international plug adapter.

If you're presenting a long way from the office and your slot is first thing in the morning, you have a choice: you can go up the night before, or catch an early train or flight on the day of the pitch. But if that train/plane is delayed, you run the risk of arriving at the pitch anxious, breathless and sweaty. Not a great start. And if you miss the train/plane altogether, you're stuffed. All those long hours and midnight oil will have been for nought.

Being prepared logistically is about controlling your environment. If possible, ask the client if you can see in advance the room you'll be presenting in, i.e. 'recce the venue'. Sketch or photograph the room; note where the plugs, doors and windows are; think about the best position for the data projector and screen (if you bring your own); ask if an IT/technical expert will be on hand.

Why is all this prep so important?
Because the more of this stuff you've squared away and dealt with, the more of your mental and physical energy you can devote to your content. And the better you know your content, the more you can focus on the people who really matter – the client panel.

DELIVERING YOUR WINNING PRESENTATION AND HANDLING THE Q&A

It's the day of the pitch, and you know what? Most of the hard work is already done.

If you've put in the hard yards up-front, you should be feeling confident and relaxed, as well as alert and ready for action. You should know your own and your colleagues' presentations inside out; you've been put through your paces by panel reviews and rehearsals; you're clear about what sort of questions to expect and which ones to answer; you've got confidence in your team-mates and in your value proposition. What's to fear?

The only things that can go wrong are:
x It's a done deal with another bidder and always has been
x The client brings in a new panel member whom you don't know
x The client moves the goal-posts on price, spec or staffing needs
x Your main ally on the panel (your 'friend at court') is called away to an urgent meeting and misses your pitch.

Everything in this list is out of your control or circle of influence, so why worry?

I'm not advocating sashaying into the pitch with a feather boa, a bottle of Bollinger and a cavalier attitude that suggests to the client you think you've already won it. No, you must be absolutely professional and disciplined. But the main reason you and your team-mates have spent valuable time prepping is to give the client a pitch that will blow them away and do it in a way that allows your natural personality and enthusiasm to come through.

In the white heat of a competitive pitch – provided you tick all the client's commercial and technical boxes – it's the soft stuff that sways the decision-makers. **Rapport, empathy, chemistry, excitement and enthusiasm turn a proficient pitch into a powerful one.**

Let's examine the personal/psychological aspect a bit closer.

A pitch is a high-energy experience, or should be, so make sure you sleep well the night before. It also pays dividends to warm your body and your voice before the pitch. Do some gentle stretches, roll your shoulders, swing your arms, touch your toes, take three or four deep, relaxing breaths. Relaxing physically will help you to relax mentally.

As for your voice, just Google 'vocal exercises' for some helpful suggestions. These include rolling your tongue around the inside of your mouth several times, sticking it out vigorously and whipping it back in, chanting mantras and tongue-twisters, and trying to kiss your ear (try it, you'll see what I mean).

If you have properly warmed up, when you stand up to speak you will sound confident and warm, rather than squeaky or reedy. Your voice box will be relaxed and open, not constricted. And you will come across to the client as calm, grounded and friendly, but authoritative and credible too.

In terms of your state of mind, you need to strike a balance between being relaxed and on your mettle, alert but not anxious, professional but not aloof or distant, engaged but not frenetic. Your performance must be stage-managed, yet with room to be spontaneous.

So although the formal presentation is orchestrated – to enable you to deliver your key messages in the limited time available – the delivery mustn't be robotic or over-scripted. That's why earlier on I recommended being clear about your messages, but not learning your presentation by heart or, worse still, reading out loud from a script.

When you are presenting, you should know your slides so well that you only need to glance either at the screen or the laptop to check that the right slide is being projected. Then, making eye contact with everyone on the client panel, you can speak directly to them, needing to look only occasionally at your notes, if at all.

TO TOGGLE OR NOT TO TOGGLE, THAT IS THE QUESTION

While on the subject, there are different views about whether to show the slide both on your computer screen and on the big screen when presenting. Some say that keeping your computer screen blank stops you being tempted to look at it too often, but I think it encourages just the sort of behaviour I've decried, i.e. arching your neck to look at the big screen.

I think you should show the slide on both screens (toggle to 'duplicate' via the F1, F5 or F7 key). The advantage is that, when necessary, you can check what's being projected or read out a quote on the slide while still facing the audience, rather than turning your head and face away from them to look up at the big screen.

Whether you're single-screen or duplicate, you need to be more interesting than your slides.

LISTENING SUPPORTIVELY

When one of your colleagues is presenting, listen actively to what they are saying, as if you were hearing it for the first time. Unfortunately, when someone's attention is elsewhere, it's obvious. There's nothing more off-putting than seeing a team member mentally drifting off to a distant planet or prepping their own presentation when a colleague is centre-stage. It's unprofessional and rude not to give them your full attention. And if I'm the client, that tells me that you left prepping your bit till the last minute or that you're not a team player, both of which I'll mark you down for.

If *you're* not interested in what they're saying, why should the client be?

The other risk of switching off once you've done your bit is that you fail to spot a concern or problem among the client panel. This might be a look of puzzlement, confusion or boredom, which you and your team-mates need to be alert to. When you're prepping, this is something you as a team must agree a policy on in advance: do you stop the presentation and ask the client if everything is OK, but run the risk of throwing your timings out? Or do you wait till the Q&A and remember to check with the client then?

My advice is that if you pick up concern during the presentation, stop presenting and deal with it there and then. If you don't, the risk is that you lose the client's attention because they're pondering something you said five minutes ago. And if it's a minor concern, most reasonable people will tell you to continue your presentation and then raise it in the Q&A.

HANDLING THE Q&A

When it comes to the Q&A, there should be very few hard questions you can't handle. My only advice is this: do not react defensively to tough or aggressive questions. Never get flustered and don't take it personally. The panel are just doing their job and stress-testing you. Rather, welcome the tough questions as a platform for showcasing your experience and expertise.

If you've ever watched the BBC programme 'Dragon's Den', the most successful entrepreneurs who get investment for their product adopt exactly that approach in answering the hardest questions. Showing you can keep your cool and that you know your stuff inside out will impress.

"They fielded the questions extremely well. They didn't take them as threats, but as an opportunity to demonstrate what they could do..."
A manufacturing client

DEBRIEF: MY ADVICE

Have one.

A couple of days after delivery but before you get the result from the client, get together as a team to review your performance. It'll still be fresh in your mind and your perception of it won't be tainted by the result.

Kick off by setting some ground rules around feedback. For instance, if views are expressed on individual performances, those comments must give the recipient evidence and information that they can apply to their next pitch.

It serves no purpose – and indeed can damage confidence and relationships – to judge a team member, especially if they already feel bad about their performance. 'I just don't like your presenting style' is destructive feedback that helps no-one. There's little the recipient can usefully do with that information.

My advice for holding a good debrief is to follow the traditional 'sandwich' approach in this order: begin with the positive ➔ share the negative ➔ remind the group of the positive, i.e. end on an upbeat note.

The positive question is straightforward: 'What went well and why?' But don't gloss over the positive just because you're itching to get stuck into the negative. For example, confining your assessment to 'David, you did a good job' is too generic and superficial. What specific observable behaviour did David exhibit that made his performance good? How could the rest of the team emulate David to improve their own performances? Make every member of the team feel good about themselves and their contribution.

As for sharing the negative, if there is any, an obvious question is 'What would you do differently next time and why?' Ask the team to assess its own performance, then give each team member the chance to assess themselves, if moved to do so. It often helps if the team captain starts this process.

When assessing the overall team performance, there's one key question that must be asked: **'Did we as a team do our absolute best to win this?'**

Close the debrief with a reminder of what each individual did well. The beauty parade is a tough call on people who may already be extremely busy with their 'day-job'. If you need to call on them again for another pitch, you want them committed to and energized about it, not going through the motions or resistant. So, even if you didn't get the business, make them feel good about their involvement.

I've seen a nice way of doing this. Focusing on one individual at a time, get everyone else on the team to write one positive thing anonymously about them on a post-it note. Gather them all up and give all the post-its to that person. Then move on to the next individual and so on, until every team member has a tidy pile of positive comments. I've known people to treasure this physical feedback throughout their careers.

Having held the debrief, if you then hear that you have won the contract, go out and celebrate! If not, at least you will have learnt from the experience. In your next pitch, you'll know what to do differently to shorten the odds of winning.

LET'S BUST SOME MYTHS

A lot of people have fixed ideas about how to pitch and present. I'd like to explode three of the most common ones:

BIG FAT MYTH #1: LOOKS MATTER.

Unless you're pitching for a model agency contract, this delusion encourages bid leaders to pick presenters who are good-looking but who may not be the logical or appropriate choice for that particular contract or client. I've never known a supplier to be appointed or rejected on the basis of physical looks.

Physical presentation and demeanour are different, however. This is about being well dressed and presentable, and adopting a body language that conveys professionalism and confidence to the client when you walk into the room.

An American client of mine is ex-military and always well turned out. He was once involved in a pitch to the US Department of Defense in

Washington, which he and his team won. When he got to know the main decision-maker during delivery of the contract, the client – also ex-military – told him that of all the bidders' shoes, his were the cleanest!

The take-home message is: **whether you like it or not, you're being judged, so be as presentable as possible.**

BIG FAT MYTH #2: NERVES ARE BAD.

First of all, don't worry if you're nervous before a pitch. In fact, worry if you're not.

Nerves are only bad if you let them cripple or paralyse you. Top performers in any field will tell you that you need some nerves. Those butterflies in the pit of your stomach tell your body and brain that you are about to perform and prime you for mental or physical exertion.

So don't waste your energy trying to suppress any nervous feelings. Accept them, go with them, and if you can, turn them into excitement and anticipation. That will raise your energy levels when you come to present.

Slow, deep breaths and gentle physical exercise on the morning of the pitch can help. But in my experience, the best remedy is to accept nerves as part of the territory, rather than resist them.

BIG FAT MYTH #3: ONLY CHARISMATIC PEOPLE PRESENT WELL.

Clients have told me time and again that what they seek in their suppliers and advisors is honest people who know their stuff and who are genuinely interested in and ambitious for their business. In fact, some clients are downright suspicious of ultra-smooth, slick, charismatic presenters – especially if their own presentational style is light-years away from that.

While very few people have a room-shaking aura (I'm told that Bill Clinton does), you do need to make an impact on the client. You need presence. Contrary to popular belief, anyone can have presence because it comes from desire.

'Presence' is simply *wanting to be there.*

If you'd rather be somewhere else or are secretly hoping that the ground will open up before it's your turn to present, you won't have much presence because mentally and spiritually you won't be present. But if you're gagging to affect the client and their organization, to blow their socks off with your presentation and ideas, and can't wait to take their questions, you'll have undeniable presence.

WINNER TAKES ALL
BOTTOM LINE

While the bid document is essentially an intellectual exercise, the pitch involves verbal and non-verbal communication, giving clients an experiential understanding of what you'll be like to work with. So, for that brief but intense hour, you and your colleagues must wield all three weapons of persuasion: credibility, logic and passion.

FOOD FOR THOUGHT

Review your latest pitch against the list below. Did you do the Dos and avoid the Don'ts?

DO	DON'T
Prep the Q&A thoroughly	Let one person dominate
Rehearse individually and collectively	React defensively to tough questions
Turn your features into benefits via 'So what?'	Talk too much about yourself
Build a killer slide that summarizes your value proposition or service model	Bombard the client with too many ideas
Let your personality come through	Bore them
Show enthusiasm	Think you can wing it
Recce the venue, if you can	Neglect any member of the panel
Bring your proposition alive with stories, quotes, physical props	Disengage when the rest of your team are presenting
Ask for the business – and mean it	Assume you've won

In your next pitch, what could you do more of, less of or stop doing altogether to raise your odds of winning? Give that some thought and note your ideas in the table below:

Do more of	
Do less of	
Stop doing altogether	

See you over the page at 'Principle 6: 'Get client feedback post-award'.

principle

6

Get client feedback post-award

WHY DOES CLIENT FEEDBACK MATTER AND HOW DO YOU GET IT?

Win, lose or draw, you must research every major proposal once the client has made their decision. Otherwise, how will you learn and improve? Your goal in conducting post-proposal research is to get candid feedback from the client on your bid. Understanding how being on the receiving end of your bid made the client think, feel and behave, and how that shaped their decision, will help you refine your approach and improve your submissions.

The key word in the paragraph above is 'candid'. Too often, clients fob us off with a vague or boilerplate response that offers no useful insight into the strengths or weaknesses of our bid. They're either scared of offending us with their candour or worried we might appeal against the decision if they disclose any dubious evaluation.

The main reason bidders get poor feedback is that the wrong people ask for it.

Most bidders send a member of the bid team either to the debriefing session or to the client interview. But if they are the very person the client happened not to like on the bid team, the client's unlikely to be open and honest about that. So it makes sense to use a third party.

At Ernst & Young, we briefed an independent research company to interview the client after every major submission. Most clients gave an hour and the researcher posed our questions, recorded the interview, transcribed it and produced a summary of the findings.

We quickly learnt what we did well, what to do differently next time and what to stop doing altogether. To us in the National Proposals team, the feedback we received was gold dust. It gave us the ammunition and the authority to spread the word of proposals best practice throughout the firm, as well as give the bid team in question feedback that they could apply to their next opportunity. It helped us to promote a culture of bidding best practice in the firm, ultimately resulting in the firm doubling its tender win-rate.

PLEASE DON'T SHOOT THE MESSENGER...
Sometimes the client's feedback was personal. I remember one occasion when the client said that the only member of the bid team he didn't like was the bid leader, a senior partner in the firm. Ouch. The client felt that he had dominated the meetings and the pitch and that his arrogance had destroyed any sense of teamwork. Despite everything else in our bid being fine, the selection panel had decided that they couldn't work with him.

It was down to me to give the partner that feedback.

I framed the client's comments as a gift to his future proposals: the client was doing him a favour in being so direct. And I couched it in terms of his observable behaviour on those occasions being perceived as arrogant, rather than labelling him an arrogant person. It was an uncomfortable experience for both of us, but to his credit he recognized that he could improve his behaviour. If nothing else, it made him more aware of how he treated his team and came across in competitive situations.

Besides getting invaluable feedback on specific bids, over time this post-proposal research grew into a wealth of insights, hints, tips, tools and techniques that we turned into a bible of best practice. Collated, professionally designed and bound, the book was compulsory reading for anyone joining the National Proposals team – or who simply wanted to win more bids, tenders and proposals.

So, if you want candid, timely feedback, it's vital that you do three things:
1. Prime the client at the outset of the bid process that at the end, when the dust has settled, you will be seeking their feedback on your bid;
2. Reassure them that your intention is not to pick holes with their evaluation or dispute their decision, but to constantly improve each bid you submit;
3. Employ a third party to conduct the interview, to distance the bid team from the process and make the client feel less defensive.

If you time this request right – when you feel you've established rapport with them, probably in the pre-submission meetings – most clients will agree to it. And telling them how you close your proposal process will show them how seriously you take it, which is likely to impress them.

If the client's feedback is negative, you may be tempted to get defensive, to discredit or dismiss it. 'They don't know what they're talking about/they're too junior/they're lying/I don't care'. Whether you agree with the feedback or not, remember that they are the buyer and their perception is your reality. It's not a matter of whether they're objectively wrong or right; it's how they experienced your bid and their interaction with you that counts.

WHAT SHOULD YOU SEEK FEEDBACK ON?

Start with their evaluation criteria. It makes sense to get their take on how you addressed what matters most to them, i.e. the key elements of your proposal that they judged you on.

The standard and most obvious criteria are:
• Your technical bid, including your proposed solution
• Your commercial bid
• Your service delivery and team
• Your ability/capacity to deliver the solution
• Your credentials.

Bear in mind that many buyers will have a template for giving feedback, so it would be politic to use that. If they don't, and your bid adopted a new, experimental approach or featured a new product or service, you may want to focus on that instead.

Figure 6.1 is a real example of candid, specific feedback from the Contracts Officer of a metropolitan local authority in the UK to a small supplier on their failed PQQ (pre-qualification questionnaire).

You can see for yourself how clear the feedback is and what the supplier will have to do the next time they submit a bid to this authority. They now know how high the bar is and what it will take to reach it.

You are probably aware that UK public sector bodies are obliged by law to give bidders the following information:
• Award criteria, i.e. which criteria and weightings governed the contract award decision
• Their total score
• The name and score of the contract winner.

Re.: Contract Number · Framework Agreement for Servicing, Inspections and Reporting Services for Fixed and Portable Fire Fighting Equipment

I write to inform you that your Pre Qualification Questionnaire was unsuccessful on this occasion. There was a great deal of interest in this contract, and we received a total of 21 applications. Your score was 7 out of 25. As detailed in the contract notice, the panel shortlisted the six highest scoring organisations for invitation to tender. The six shortlisted organisations scored between 13 and 18.

The areas where your application could have scored higher are as follows:

- 2.1 did not give values for past contracts. More explanation was needed on the examples given, particularly in relation to timely service delivery and how this was achieved.
- 2.2 made no mention of complaint resolution or effective communication. Detail was needed on the processes and procedures in place.
- 2.3 did not provide evidence of your organisation's health and safety record. More detail was needed in order to meet the requirements of the question.
- 2.4 gave little information. Environmental and sustainability policies were referred to, but no detail was given as to what these policies involve, or how they have been implemented.
- 2.5 made no mention of legal requirements or staff retention, which were points specifically raised in the question. Other point were covered, but required more detail.

Thank you for your efforts and interest in working for   Council. Please do not let this deter you from applying for any other suitable arrangements in the future.

FIGURE 6.1. Sample feedback from a UK local authority. Detailed feedback on the bidders' scores helps organizations improve their submissions.

THE UK PUBLIC SECTOR 'STANDSTILL PERIOD'

If you are unsuccessful in a public sector tender and decide to challenge the award decision, you can use the 'standstill period' to do so. This is a mandatory 10-day pause between notification of the awarding of the contract and the signing of the contract with the winning supplier. Also known as the 'Alcatel Period', due to a court case involving that company, this small window of time allows bidders to get more information about the award decision if they feel they have been harshly dealt with.

A legal requirement that all public authorities must comply with, the standstill applies to all procurements covered by the full scope of the European Union (EU) Procurement Directives. In other words, it applies to all EU contracts equalling or exceeding a certain financial value for supplies, services or works (see *EU thresholds* in the glossary of terms for the current levels).

FREEDOM OF INFORMATION

If you miss the standstill period deadline or are still unhappy with the feedback provided by the contracting authority, you can submit a Freedom of Information (FOI) request. The Freedom of Information Act 2000

gives the UK public right of access to information held by public authorities in two ways:
- Public authorities must publish certain information about their activities.
- Members of the public are entitled to request information from those authorities.

Simply send a written request (email is OK) to the Information Officer at the relevant authority, who is obliged by law to respond within 20 working days. Of course, there's no guarantee that the authority will release the information you ask for, especially if they deem it to be commercially or legally sensitive. But those exemptions are rare.

Under an FOI request, you should be able to get the score, ranking and evaluation comments of your own PQQ and bid, plus a summary of why you were unsuccessful. As you might expect, information about the other bidders and their bids tends to be off-limits.

FIND OUT WHY YOU WON, TOO
As Anthony Robbins says in *Awaken the Giant Within*, 'When we win we tend to party; when we lose we tend to ponder.'

Winning bidders are usually too busy celebrating or going into delivery mode to ask why they won. But once the Bollinger (or the Prosecco, depending on the value of the win) has stopped fizzing, find out why you won. That way you know what to reproduce next time or do even better.

It's also much easier to get feedback on a win than on a loss: the client knows you're unlikely to dispute their decision! And as you'll be working together to deliver the contract, they'll be open with you.

HOW SHOULD YOU APPLY WHAT YOU LEARN FROM THE CLIENT?
The most effective way to embed the learning is to share it with the bid team in the 'wash-up' meeting or internal debrief, then add it to your pro-posals 'library', if you have one. The wash-up meeting is an essential final step in the tendering process, where you assess your own performance and overlay it on the feedback from the client. Sadly, most organizations fail to hold a structured debrief at the end of the process. Why? Either be-cause the bid team rush back to their day-jobs (which they've neglected in order to work on the tender) or they're already onto the next bid (they've become a proposals factory).

The broad questions you want to ask and answer in the wash-up meeting are:
'What did we do well?'

'What could we do differently or better next time?'

'Who's going to make sure we apply those improvements/lessons learnt to the next bid?'

You could map a simple matrix onto your process to analyse each stage of the proposal, to create a 'bid improvement plan' for your bid team:

PROPOSAL STAGE	WHAT WENT WELL	WHAT DIDN'T GO SO WELL	IMPROVEMENT IDEAS / LESSONS LEARNT	WHO WILL DO WHAT BY WHEN
Pre-qualification				
Team selection				
Pre-submission client meetings				
Bid document				
Beauty parade				
Post-proposal research				

Improvement ideas can range from building a library of model responses to standard tender questions and pre-qualifying opportunities better, faster mobilisation, more robust team selection and better-prepared pitches.

Much of the feedback I've talked about so far in this chapter is qualitative and subjective; it tends to be the 'soft' stuff. But it's also important to look at the harder metrics and measure your bidding performance quantitatively too.

KEEPING SCORE: HOW TO TRACK YOUR TENDERING PROGRESS

For me, the most valuable metric is the return on investment (ROI) of your tendering activity. This measures the profitability or cost-effectiveness of your tendering.

ROI is usually applied to investment decisions, but I see no reason why we can't also use it to evaluate tendering activity. In the same way that investors want to know that the return generated by a financial instrument will be greater than the original cost of that investment, we need to know that our resource-hungry tenders will generate a return for us, i.e. that they're worth all the blood, sweat and, occasionally, tears.

The standard ROI formula is:

$$\text{Return on investment} = \frac{\text{gain from investment less cost of investment}}{\text{cost of investment}}$$

So how do you calculate your tendering ROI? Here's my six-step, back-of-the-envelope formula:

1. DEFINE YOUR SCOPE.
Will you include all bids, i.e. single, non-competitive proposals and re-proposals, or just competitive tenders for new clients that followed a formal process? Does your scope include or exclude PQQs?

2. CHOOSE YOUR TIME-FRAME.
What period will your measurement cover? You need a time-frame that will include enough tenders to give you meaningful data, like a financial or calendar year.

3. CALCULATE THE TOTAL VALUE OF ALL NEW CONTRACTS WON BY TENDER IN THAT TIME-FRAME.
This is the total revenue value to your organization over the lifetime of each contract.

4. CALCULATE THE TOTAL COST OF ALL TENDERING ACTIVITY IN THAT TIME-FRAME.
This should include all your staff time and material costs, like printing and design, research, travel and accommodation for all the contracts covered in step 3. What did it cost you to win them? This figure is the cost of your investment.

(Some people think you should also include your 'opportunity cost' when calculating your tendering investment. This is the cost of missing out on other opportunities or neglecting existing clients because you diverted resources into the tenders whose ROI you're measuring.

Though this is virtually impossible to quantify, one thing is certain: tendering for major contracts has an opportunity cost, meaning that your actual ROI is probably lower than you think. Yet another reason to pre-qualify every opportunity.)

5. SUBTRACT YOUR FIGURE IN STEP 4 FROM YOUR FIGURE IN STEP 3.

The resulting number is the gross profit of your tendering activity.

6. DIVIDE YOUR FIGURE IN STEP 5 BY YOUR FIGURE IN STEP 4.

The resulting number is your ROI.

For instance, if you won £100,000 worth of new business in a certain period and you spent £10,000 on the tenders to win it, you'd have an ROI of 9 or 900% (100,000 – 10,000 => 90,000 / 10,000). In other words, every £1 you spent tendering generated a return of £9. Your organization needs to agree a target ROI zone or range. Clearly, if your investment is greater than your return, something's wrong!

Win-rate might be easier to calculate...
As you can see, calculating your ROI is no simple matter.

A simpler metric is to work out your win-rate, i.e. what proportion you win of the total number of tenders you respond to. This is usually expressed as a ratio, e.g. 1 in 3 (1:3), or as a percentage.

Provided you're comparing like with like, it's important to track your win-rate: you need to know if you're getting better or worse. And you can measure win-rates for different aspects of your tendering. For example, you can compare the performance of different business units or teams across different geographies or service lines.

A falling win-rate should prompt some organizational soul-searching:

'Are we going for the wrong opportunities?'

'Are we over-bidding?'

'Are we submitting lower-quality bids?'

'Is our proposals team overworked and stale?'

'Are we choosing the wrong bid teams?'

'Has our reputation been damaged?'

'Is the market changing? Do we understand the new market dynamics?'

'Is price even more of an issue than usual? Can we be smarter about pricing?'

Whatever your answers to these questions, if your win-rate (and therefore your ROI) is going south, you will need to change some element(s) of your sales and tendering activity to stop the rot. If you've read this far, you should already have learnt some practical ways of doing that.

Measuring customer satisfaction

Another metric to consider is customer satisfaction. Your primary customer is, of course, external: the buyer(s) in the client organization. If you play a bid support role, you may also want to measure the satisfaction levels of your internal customers, like the fee-earners on the bid team, as well as functions such as Finance, HR, Compliance and IT.

Getting regular feedback from them through surveys, focus groups, interviews and other research tools on what it was like working with you is useful. In the interests of continuously improving, it gives you insight into the strengths, weaknesses and perceptions of you and your performance, and shows them that you take customer service seriously. Provided, of course, that you act on the feedback and are seen to do so, it will also strengthen your relationship with them.

WINNER TAKES ALL
BOTTOM LINE

Whatever you measure, establish an accurate baseline first.
That way you'll know if your tendering performance
and ROI are getting better or worse.

FOOD FOR THOUGHT

Try responding to the following statements by putting a big, bold X in the appropriate column:

YOUR ORGANIZATION...	NOT SURE	YES/AGREE	NO/DISAGREE
...has a clear, documented process for seeking post-proposal feedback from the client			
...captures client feedback that you can apply appropriately to your next bid			
...holds a formal, agenda'd 'wash-up' review at the end of every major tender where people are held accountable for implementing improvement ideas			
...tracks its tendering ROI systematically			
...tracks its tender win-rate systematically			

If you put an X in the last column ('No/disagree') for any of the statements, chances are your proposal closure process is not serving you as well as it could.

Given how onerous but potentially lucrative tendering can be, you owe it to yourself and your staff to keep track of how you're doing, both internally and from a client perspective.

Think of your proposal closure process as an early warning system: if you're investing valuable, finite resources in bids with questionable returns, you want to know sooner rather than later, so you can course-correct quickly and become the business development powerhouse you know you can be!

See you overleaf for the seventh and final principle: 'Manage the bid like a project'.

principle

7

Manage the bid like a project

CHAPTER SUMMARY

1. The bid manager's role.
2. Knowledge: what must a bid manager know?
3. Skills: what must bid managers know how to do?
4. Attitudes: which ones do bid managers need?
5. Where does bid management end and internal consulting begin?
6. How do bid managers get the respect they deserve?

THE BID MANAGER'S ROLE

Of all the roles in a tender, the bid or proposal manager's is probably the hardest and surely one of the most important. Typically part of an organization's central bid support team or dedicated to the bids of a particular product/service line or practice group, they manage the internal logistics and moving parts of the bid process, effectively acting as the project manager. They make the bid happen.

If they fall down on the job, the whole process falls apart, with disastrous consequences. Clients pick up on poor internal organization; some will even score you on it. For instance, if you're slow out of the blocks in asking for meetings or posing clarification questions, or if you submit your bid too close to the deadline, the client may mark you down. **So a bid manager can make or break a bid.**

And that's why they must manage the bid like a project.

Like a project, a bid has an output (the bid document or presentation); an outcome (contract award); prescribed timescales (clarification window, submission date); internal milestones (kick-off and review meetings, document drafts, rehearsals, presentation etc); a scope (defined by the spec and the ITT/RFP); and it requires stakeholder management (the bid team and other contributors to the bid).

So the bid manager should drive the process with a realistic timetable that everyone involved buys into, with agreed milestones, deadlines, deliverables and accountabilities, ensuring that every stakeholder in the bid understands what is expected of them, why and when.

Where bid management differs from project management, however, is in the value that the best bid managers can add to a bid in terms of shaping its content and getting the best out of the bid team. And that's where good bid managers must field an awesome array of knowledge, skills and attitudes.

KNOWLEDGE: WHAT MUST A BID MANAGER KNOW?

If you're a bid manager, you need to understand proposals best practice, so you can guide the bid team in the right direction. Demonstrating this knowledge gives you credibility with the bid team, making it likelier that they will listen to you and follow your advice. Citing effective approaches, experience from previous bids and insights into client needs will win you brownie points with the team.

You must also know where to find relevant material for the bid. These range from corporate policy documents and certificates (especially for public sector PQQs) to relevant case studies and latest CVs. If you have access to an electronic proposals library where all this core material is gathered in one place, great. If not, you may find yourself reinventing the wheel.

You clearly need to know your own organization, the key players and stakeholders in it, what it does, what makes it different or special, its USP, its strategy. The larger your organization, the harder this is.

You also need to know the client and, if possible, the competition. Even if you don't do the actual desktop research yourself but delegate it to your library services or knowledge management function (if you have one), you will probably be the conduit for distributing that information to the team. When it comes to championing the client's viewpoint, you will need to understand their business and what commercial, organizational, political or economic issues are driving the tender.

On a practical level, you need to know how to plan, structure, draft and edit a powerful bid document, as well as brief and edit other people's contributions. So knowledge of grammar, punctuation and overall business style, document design and management – much of which we covered in Principle 4, 'Persuade through the written word' – is essential.

If there is a beauty parade, you also need to understand what constitutes a good presentation, how best to help the team prepare and when to recommend an external pitch coach or consultant, if you find the team's needs exceed your own experience or capabilities. It helps if you already know the team members.

You need to know yourself, too. Your strengths are important, of course, but you need to know your weaknesses so you don't let them scupper the process. A game-critical weakness might be non-assertiveness, disorganization or panic under pressure. The risk of being in denial about a weakness is that it may show up under pressure and stress the team when they are already stretched. Recognizing your weaknesses and adopting strategies either to mask them, manage them or make up for them takes emotional intelligence and maturity.

Finally, knowing how to interact with the bid team is key. Dealing with different personalities in the white heat of a tendering process – including bid team members who are more senior than you – brings its own pressure. The more thought you give to their individual styles and how best to communicate with them and get on their wavelength, the more you'll get out of them. You might want to refer back to Principle 2, 'Choose the best team' to remind yourself of the four basic motivational styles of Carer, Driver, Professional and Adapter and their influence on behaviour.

SKILLS: WHAT MUST BID MANAGERS KNOW HOW TO DO?

A good bid manager needs a jamboree of skills, which can be grouped under three headings: Communication (written and oral); Management; and Organization.

COMMUNICATION	MANAGEMENT	ORGANIZATION
Persuade busy people to contribute to the bid	Manage the bid timetable (e.g. pre-empt roadblocks, barriers and dependencies)	Establish a bid timetable
Communicate clearly both orally and in writing	Manage detail (while holding the big picture in your head)	Work effectively to a deadline
Plan, draft, edit and produce bid documents under pressure	Facilitate/co-lead meetings with the bid leader	

Organize meetings, briefings, debriefings, panel reviews, rehearsals and coordinate multiple participants		
Review and summarize long, complex documents (e.g. the ITT / RFP)	Motivate (and occasionally prod) staff to deliver text on time	Estimate realistically how long a task will take
Get on with people, regardless of their role or position	Manage multiple versions of a document	Be able to organize yourself and others
Help develop messages, win-themes and benefits	Delegate upwards (to a more senior stakeholder in the bid)	
Create text based on an outline brief or conversation	Brief internal and external resources (e.g. Subject Matter Experts (SMEs), graphic designers, consultants / coaches, writers, editors, desktop publishers, printers)	
Edit someone else's text (and justify your edits)		
Answer non-technical questions in the bid document		

To be a good bid manager, I believe you need to be proficient in all three areas.

ATTITUDE: WHICH ONES DO BID MANAGERS NEED?

- Positive, can-do
- Energetic but calm
- Flexible, adaptable
- Patient (but not a pushover)
- Persistent, determined
- Professional, i.e. demanding high standards of themselves and others
- Objective, realistic
- Resilient, i.e. doesn't wilt under pressure
- Creative
- Assertive, but not aggressive
- Confident
- Treat their internal stakeholders as external clients
- Committed and motivated to win.

And the King of these? For me, it's the last bullet, 'Committed and motivated to win'. If your bid manager has that burning desire and is gagging to do what it takes to win, they're much more likely to have the other attributes too – or at least be prepared to develop them. But if their heart's not truly in it, they'll just be going through the motions and won't run that extra mile either for the bid or the bid team.

I met a bid manager like that once. Within seconds of being introduced, I sensed he was the wrong person for the role. I got negative 'vibes' from him; he had one of those auras that seemed to drain energy rather than generate it. He had a low-energy, unassuming, non-assertive personality whose body language (slumped in his chair, semi-scowling!) betrayed his mindset. He was full of 'atti'. At first I thought it was me, that he was reacting to my being brought in to the bid by his MD and he'd interpreted that as implicit criticism of him. I imagined he was thinking something like 'Damned consultant muscling in on my patch...'.

But over the next few weeks of working with him, I realized that he possessed hardly any of the above attitudes. He wasn't a monster or a bad person, and it was nothing to do with me; that's just how he was. But I felt duty bound to mention my concern discreetly to the MD, who acknowledged there was a problem. The truth was that, with him, our chances of winning were much lower than without him. Fortunately, he recognized he was in the wrong job and by mutual consent soon left the organization. (We managed to rescue the bid at the 11th hour, but it was touch and go.)

I talked a moment ago about 'going the extra mile', but in bids and tenders it may only be inches. A bid manager's ability to get the best out of people, sometimes more senior than themselves, comes from understanding that the margin between winning and losing a tender can be as little as half a percentage point or a fraction of a mark.

To continue the sporting analogy, the British Cycling Team swept the medals board in the 2012 London Olympics by making small improvements to every aspect of their performance. Besides the obvious gruelling training, this ranged from developing tyres that could be pumped a few millibars harder than their rivals and spending hours in a wind tunnel to refine their body position on the bike, to sleeping in the right position and on the same pillow when they were away from home.

The British Cycling Team leader, Dave Brailsford, explained: "The whole principle came from the idea that if you broke down everything you could think of that goes into riding a bike, and then improved it by 1%, you'd get a big increase when you put them all together."

They called this the 'marginal gains theory'… and tenders are no different. When competing at the highest level for a lucrative contract where award decisions are often made on the tiniest margins, the best bid managers and their teams should pay similar attention to every detail of the process.

WHERE DOES BID MANAGEMENT END AND INTERNAL CONSULTING BEGIN?

The top bid managers go beyond simply managing the logistics of the internal bid process and add value to the bid itself, influencing the client's experience of it. The four dimensions of a bid that good bid managers must handle simultaneously I see as a compass:

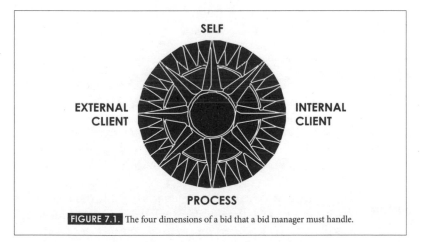

SELF

EXTERNAL CLIENT

INTERNAL CLIENT

PROCESS

FIGURE 7.1. The four dimensions of a bid that a bid manager must handle.

At magnetic North, the bid manager must manage themselves and their behaviour. This is about managing their impact on and relationship with the bid team, their energy levels, personability, presentability, language and overall professionalism.

Moving clockwise to due East, they must support their internal customer, especially the bid leader. This involves establishing themselves as a vital support to the team by adding immediate value from day 1, e.g. asking probing questions, challenging assumptions, summarizing the ITT/RFP and pulling out key requirements, creating a compliance matrix, reminding the team of proposals best practice, editing first draft text.

Due South is about managing the logistics of the process, so that it flows smoothly and everyone is clear about what's expected of them. The bid manager must be on top of every aspect of whatever step of the process they're at. This is where a split-screen mind comes in: they hold the big picture of the bid alongside meticulous attention to detail. They must drive the process and be seen to do so.

The fourth dimension lies in the West, where they can add value by championing the client's viewpoint and making the bid team reflect on the buyer's experience. 'How are they feeling about us?' 'Where else can we add value for them?' 'What do they think of us?' 'Is our team right for them?' 'Are we on the right track?' 'Do we still think this is winnable?' can provoke changes of tack or direction. This is where the bid manager needs the confidence to challenge the team, provided it's in the ultimate interests of the bid.

THE HIGHS AND LOWS OF A BID MANAGER

THE LOW

Jim started his professional life as a junior BD executive in a law firm. One day he was invited to work on a 'game-changing' opportunity, providing legal services to a large investment fund. But the partner who'd received the ITT and who knew the client well decided he didn't have the time or resources to invest in it.

The ITT comprised only 12 questions, but the partner's attitude was: 'Oh, just fill them in, I know what they want, it'll be fine. It's ours to lose.' Jim cobbled together a response, which the partner cast his eye over and signed off. Despite scoring badly on the written response, the firm was invited to present. The same thing happened. The partner was so convinced they had it in the bag that the team didn't practise their presentation, with the inevitable result that they lost.

When they attended the client debrief, the feedback was damning. The 'document was poor, it looked cut and pasted, lacked creativity and imagination. As for the presentation, it was shambolic. You clearly weren't bothered'. The partner was stunned. But there was a silver lining. The internal analysis of what had gone wrong triggered wholesale change in how the firm responds to major opportunities.

THE HIGH

Some months later, despite the earlier debacle, Jim's firm was invited to tender to another division of the same client organization. This time he worked with a partner who cleared her diary for a week within minutes of the client call. She was clearly committed to the process and to winning, inspiring Jim to give his best. The document he helped the team produce was relevant, concise and creative, and scored highly in the client evaluation. So far, so good.

Under the committed leadership of the partner, Jim helped the team develop three simple win-themes for the presentation. With only 40 minutes for both presentation and Q&A, on a complex legal solution to a panel that included non-legal people, they placed huge physical jigsaw pieces on the table to show how all the elements of their solution fitted together. If any single piece was missing or neglected, the solution wouldn't work.

The client loved it and they won the contract.

HOW DO BID MANAGERS GET THE RESPECT THEY DESERVE?
LET ME KICK THIS OFF WITH A STORY.

A bid manager had just joined a law firm and was introduced to the senior partner. "Trevor, this is Paul. He's just started with us as a bid manager on the BD team." "Oh, an overhead," retorted the senior partner, turned on his heels and walked off.

How does the central bid or proposals function in an organization get more respect from fee-earners? How does the BD director get a seat at the top table?

I see BD teams around the world under-valued by their organization. There are several reasons why:

* They've allowed themselves to become glorified administrators or expensive secretaries
* The fee-earners don't appreciate how hard bid management is
* Some fee-earners don't value marketing and sometimes confuse it with business development
* The head of BD and/or their team are poor at promoting/defending the value they add

✗ They've recruited the wrong people
✗ They've recruited the right people, but they're doing the wrong things.

Besides mastering the skills, knowledge and attitudes I've described in this chapter, bid managers need to take the time and trouble to build long-term relationships with their internal stakeholders, just as they would with an external client if they were client-facing.

And that can be fun. It doesn't have to be a chore or a bore.

One of the most successful people I ever worked with was a fellow consultant at PricewaterhouseCoopers. Most of the time Howard was to be found either in the local pub or a restaurant, spending time with colleagues, prospects or clients. He pulled in more business than virtually anyone else... and managed to do so without hurting his liver. He enjoyed their company, and on the odd occasion he didn't, he made sure they enjoyed his.

My point here is not to encourage you to become a feckless lush who falls into a drunken stupor after lunch (RIP those days of boozy lunches), but to spend time building solid relationships with your internal, bid team customers. Those relationships will pay dividends when you need their engagement on and commitment to a bid.

By mastering the 'hard' skills of managing a bid like a project and the 'soft' skills of communications and relationship-building, you will add huge value to the bid, reinforce the credibility of your organization's business development function... and win more bids, tenders and proposals.

WINNER TAKES ALL
BOTTOM LINE

If BD and all who sail in her want the respect they deserve, they need to do more than simply manage the bid process. They must be more than project managers. Their role must be to support and challenge the team in equal measure and influence the structure, content and delivery of a winning bid.

FOOD FOR THOUGHT

We've come to the end of our brief journey through the 7 ½ trusted principles of proposals best practice. But I don't want you to close the book, stick it on your bookshelf (unless, of course, you're reading the e-book) and forget about it. I want it to become a well-thumbed, dog-eared, coffee-stained book that you refer to every time you start work on a bid.

Please take some time now to skim back over the principles, reminding yourself of a good idea here, a novel approach there, or those places in the margin where you've noted something of interest.

Now think about what aspects of tendering you're good at and write them down in the left-hand column, without limit. Revel in those strengths. Congratulate yourself on being good at that stuff. Be proud of them and don't under-value them.

Now think about what you'd like to be better at and rank the top three. You may want to analyse an ITT/RFP faster, write more concise bid answers, be a more effective presentation coach, or learn to be more assertive with senior people. Rank them in the order that will have the greatest impact on the bids you work on.

Finally, when you've done that, brainstorm some ways you could achieve those top three improvements. Could you go on a training course, hire a coach, read a book, talk to an expert? Build a simple plan for improving those three aspects of your tendering toolkit, with a time-frame allotted to each. Then implement the plan!

Aspects of tendering I'm good at	
3 aspects of tendering I want to be better at	1. 2. 3.
What I can do to achieve the above	

EPILOGUE

Once upon a time, I worked with an ambitious, hard-nosed corporate finance partner called Laura. She was a tough operator, both with her clients and internally, but she won every tender she went for.

One day we were chatting about a bid and she came out with something that shocked me:

> *"You know, Scott, this may surprise you, but the key to winning tenders is showing your clients love."*

My face must have been a picture because she laughed, then explained:

> *"I know, it sounds a bit New Agey, doesn't it? Don't get me wrong. Price, method, approach, all the techie stuff has to be right, but the more deeply you care about your client, their business and their success, the more they'll love you back.*
>
> *"Also, it's a funny thing, but the deeper you care, the more of yourself and your creativity you invest in the bid. When that happens, you'll find that innovative solutions to their problems just come to you, almost without trying.*
>
> *"But when your heart's not in it and you just go through the motions, you produce a response that's functional and lifeless – and the client reacts accordingly. It's like anything else in life: you get out what you put in."*

She paused briefly, as if summoning her vast experience.

> *"Of course, you can do all that… and you still might not win. It's a buyer's market; there are no guarantees. But if you have a genuine desire to communicate with the client and truly help them, you'll shorten the odds big-time."*

When I consider the range of knowledge, skills and attitudes needed to be good at bids…

When I consider the skill needed to blend project management with internal consulting…

When I consider the persistence, patience and perceptiveness needed to take a bid to the next level…

When I consider what it takes to get the client to choose you above all other bidders…

When I consider how hard it can be to sit up all night with your bid colleagues and still smile in the morning…

When I recall how wonderful it is to hear that the client has awarded you the contract…

When I consider all this – whether you're a novice bid executive, a mid-career bid manager or a seasoned bid director – wherever you are in the world, I salute you.

To close, I'm moved to recall the words of Vince Lombardi, the flamboyant, perfectionist Head Coach and General Manager of the Green Bay Packers American football team in the 1960s, who had the Super Bowl trophy named after him when he died:

"WINNING ISN'T EVERYTHING. IT'S THE **ONLY THING!**"

GLOSSARY OF TENDERING TERMS

Beauty parade: formal, face-to-face presentation by shortlisted suppliers to a client panel, usually after submission of the bid document. This is the supplier's last opportunity to influence the client's decision. Often referred to as a 'pitch' in media and advertising, and an 'interview' in professional services.

Best practice: considered the best way to perform a task or activity. 'Proposals best practice' refers to a range of behaviours, knowledge and skills that represent the most effective way of winning business proposals.

Bid: a formal written offer or quote made by a supplier/bidder to deliver the contract specified by the *buyer* in the tender documentation. The bid document typically includes the bidder's understanding of the client's situation/needs/goals, the bidder's proposed solution/value proposition (including price), bidder credentials/customer references, and next steps.

Bidder: a supplier that bids for a contract in response to an *ITT* or *RFP*. Interchangeable with *Tenderer*.

Business development (BD): an organizational function responsible for growing the business, both through cross-selling to existing clients and selling to new ones. In most organizations, this function includes submitting proposals and responding to *ITTs/RFPs*, or supporting practice groups/business units to do so. In other organizations, 'BD' also includes activities more commonly associated with marketing, e.g. PR, events, sponsorship and advertising.

Business Process Outsourcing (BPO): an outsourcing relationship where a third-party provider (a *Managed Service Provider*, or *MSP*) takes over and runs a client's business processes. For example, a company may outsource its HR or recruitment function. In the latter example, a third party assumes the role of the client's recruiting department by owning and being accountable for its recruitment processes.

Business questionnaire: what some local/municipal authorities (e.g. Lambeth in south London) call a *PQQ* (Pre-Qualification Questionnaire), i.e. the first step in the two-step *'restricted'* public sector procurement procedure.

Buyer: an organization that specifies a purchasing need and puts a tender out to market, to receive bids from interested bidders/suppliers. Also referred to as the 'client'.

Contracting authority: the formal term for the buyer or buying organization in UK public sector tenders.

CPV codes: Common Procurement Vocabulary codes are a standardized system of classifying public sector contract opportunities in the *Official Journal of the European Union (OJEU)* by defining the subject of each contract. CPV codes allow potential suppliers to trawl easily through the many thousands of opportunities to find the most relevant ones to their business.

EOI: Expression of Interest. Often the first step in the tendering process, suppliers express their interest in tendering for a contract. Public sector contracting organizations (i.e. the *buyer*) may ask suppliers for outline information about their company at this stage.

e-Tendering: the electronic version of the procurement process, i.e. supplier registration/expression of interest, contract download, submission of bid document, evaluation of tenders, all done online. It may or may not involve an e-auction (also known as 'reverse auction').

EU thresholds: financial levels or limits relating to the estimated lifetime value of a public sector contract. Where the value of a contract equals or exceeds the relevant threshold, the *contracting authority* must advertise the contract in the *Official Journal of the European Union (OJEU)* and follow the procedures set out in the *Public Contracts Regulations*. Contracting authorities can also divide the contract into smaller chunks called 'lots', but no more than 20% of the contract can be let this way. The EU reviews the thresholds every two years. The current thresholds (effective from 1 January 2018) in euros, net of VAT, are: (PTO)

CONTRACTING AUTHORITY	'SUPPLIES' (goods, products, commodities)	'SERVICES' (e.g. transport, health & social services, education/training)	'WORKS' (capital projects, e.g. construction, civil engineering)
Central Government bodies[1]	€144,000	€144,000[2]	€5,548,000
Other public sector bodies	€221,000	€221,000	€5,548,000
Small lots, all bodies	€80,000	€80,000	€1,000,000

[1] Schedule 1 of the Public Contracts Regulations 2006 lists the central government bodies in the UK subject to the World Trade Organization's (WTO) Government Procurement Agreement (GPA).

[2] Except for certain services, like Research & Development, TV, radio and telecoms, which have a threshold of €200,000.

Note that utilities contracts have their own set of thresholds, governed by the Utilities Contracts Regulations 2006.

For more information on thresholds: https://www.ojec.com/thresholds.

Framework agreement: an umbrella agreement between a buyer and a supplier setting out the terms, conditions and prices of future contracts ('call-offs'). A form of supplier pre-selection or approved supplier list, it saves the buyer issuing a new tender every time they need to procure something. However, it neither commits the buyer to buying nor guarantees the supplier a sale.

Goods: physical products provided by a supplier, e.g. stationery, chairs, construction materials, IT equipment.

Incumbent: the existing provider of a contract to a client. Incumbents are often required to formally re-bid or re-tender for the contract, instead of it automatically renewing at expiry.

Invitation to tender (ITT): a document issued by the buying organization that invites shortlisted suppliers to tender for a contract. Interested suppliers respond to that invitation by submitting a bid document or tender response, becoming competitive bidders.

KPI: Key Performance Indicator. Important set of measures by which the client will assess your bid (and your performance in fulfilling the contract). In certain entrepreneurial circles, KPI is also known as Key Person of Influence, i.e. the 'go-to' person in their industry.

Low-ball: pricing a bid or tender very low – sometimes even at a loss – to win the contract. Also known as 'buying the contract'.

Mind-map: a non-linear technique for mapping information using words, pictures, shapes and colours. Useful for capturing the output of brainstorming sessions and for planning documents. Developed by Tony ('lateral thinking') Buzan.

Most economically advantageous tender (MEAT): a process for assessing public sector bids, where the evaluators take into account factors other than or in addition to price (e.g. quality, technical merit and running costs). Also known as 'best value' or 'value for money'. If MEAT is used, the contract award criteria must be set out either in the *OJEU* notice or the tender documents, and the weighting of each criterion given, either as an exact number or as a meaningful range (e.g. 'Price: 30%-40%'). In the US, the government procurement equivalent of MEAT is LPTA: Lowest Price Technically Acceptable. This is where the buyer will award the contract to the lowest bid that meets their minimum requirements.

Managed Service Provider (MSP): a company that takes on responsibility for managing another organization's business processes, e.g. HR, recruitment. This is referred to as a *Business Process Outsourcing (BPO)* model. For instance, a recruitment MSP would manage, track and report on all temporary staffing, select and manage recruitment suppliers, distribute orders and manage billing.

NDA: Non-Disclosure Agreement, signed by a supplier, who promises to keep confidential any commercially sensitive information that the client may share with them in the course of delivering a contract or assignment.

Official Journal of the European Union (OJEU): an online publication that publishes all public sector contract opportunities whose value equals or exceeds certain *EU thresholds*.

Pitch: a formal, face-to-face presentation to the client of your proposed solution or value proposition. In professional services, this is often referred to as the 'interview'.

Pre-qualification questionnaire (PQQ): the first hurdle in the UK public sector 'Restricted' tender procedure used by *contracting authorities* to shortlist eligible suppliers. PQQs typically seek information on the supplier's financial standing, track record and ability to deliver the specified contract. Suppliers satisfying those criteria are then invited, through an *invitation to tender (ITT)*, to submit a formal *tender response*.

Procurement: describes an activity or department whereby an organization buys goods, works and services from outside suppliers.

Proposal: also known as a 'business proposal'. A sales document written by a supplier to a buyer, proactively proposing a product or service. In contrast with a formal competitive tender that is initiated by the *buyer*, in a proposal scenario the initiative often comes from the supplier. The proposal is usually based on prior contact with or knowledge of that organization; in many cases, the *buyer* may already be a client of the supplier. A proposal is typically non-competitive: it may lead to a contract without any other suppliers being involved.

Public Contracts Regulations 2006 (amended 2009): legislation governing how public sector contracts above the *EU-set thresholds* in England, Wales and Northern Ireland are procured. Public sector procurement in Scotland is covered by the Public Contracts Regulations (Scotland) 2006.

Request for information (RFI): a preliminary step in the procurement process, where the client requests general information from suppliers about their organization, before deciding if they qualify for an *RFP* or an RFQ (Request for Quote).

Request for proposal (RFP): an invitation issued by the buying organization to suppliers, inviting them to bid for a specific contract or piece of work. Interchangeable with *ITT.*

Restricted procedure: a two-step UK public sector procedure for procuring supplies and services. Step 1: each supplier completes a pre-selection *Pre-Qualification Questionnaire (PQQ)* that assesses their suitability for the contract (e.g. financial standing, capacity, track record). Step 2: the *contracting authority* (public sector buyer) invites a limited number of respondents to tender.

Return on investment (ROI): a measure of the profitability of tendering activity, ROI expresses the relationship between your cost of tendering and the number/value of contracts you win. The higher the ROI, the more cost-effective your tenders.

Storyboard: a graphic technique for outlining the contents of a document or presentation in a series of sketches or picture boards (see *mind-map*).

Sustainable development: sometimes defined as 'meeting the needs of the current generation without compromising the life-quality of later generations'. Much in vogue in public sector procurement.

Tender: also known as 'competitive tender'. A formal, competitive process usually initiated by the Procurement function of an organization to put a contract or piece of work out to market. The purpose is to obtain offers from outside suppliers to deliver that contract. This can range from office stationery and furniture to a new IT system, from recruiting temporary staff to a major construction project. The word *tender* means simply to 'offer', as in 'tender your resignation' or the phrase 'legal tender'.

Tender response: the supplier's written response to the buyer's *ITT* or *RFP*, returned ('submitted') by a set date and time. This document typically includes the bidder's understanding of the client's situation/needs/goals, the bidder's proposed solution/value proposition (including price), bidder credentials/customer references, and next steps.

Tier 1 supplier: an organization at the top of the supply chain supplying goods or services directly to the client; also known as the 'main contractor'. Typically sub-contracts jobs/tasks to lower tiers of the supply chain. Common term in the construction industry.

Value proposition: a business or marketing statement that summarizes why a buyer should buy your product or service and the clear benefits of doing so. Also known as your 'offering', 'promise' or 'solution'. Value propositions can include your particular approach to the client's problem, your proposed team and price. The strongest value propositions make an explicit link between what you propose charging the client and what they will get in return.

Works: usually relates to construction, demolition or civil engineering contracts.

ABOUT THE AUTHOR

SCOTT KEYSER

Scott is a bid consultant, author and writing skills trainer who helps organizations around the world to compete more effectively for business and win 'must-win' contracts.

His background includes eight years with Ernst & Young (now EY) and PricewaterhouseCoopers. As a National Proposals Consultant with Ernst & Young in London, he helped the UK firm to double its tender win rate.

Besides training in bid writing and pitching, Scott offers clients live bid support: he works with the bid team on a live opportunity to tip the odds in their favour through hands-on help, advice and coaching.

Scott also trains professional services firms, including three Magic Circle law firms and two of the Big Four accountancy firms, in his 21 rhetorica® persuasive writing techniques. His second book, *rhetorica® – a toolkit of 21 everyday writing techniques*, is available on Amazon.

WWW.WRITEFORRESULTS.COM

25TH
LID
ANNIVERSARY

Sharing knowledge since 1993

WITHDRAWN

- 1993 Madrid
- 2008 Mexico DF and Monterrey
- 2010 London
- 2011 New York and Buenos Aires
- 2012 Bogotá
- 2014 Shanghai